CRITICAL ESSAYS 01

NIGHT

William Shakespeare

Editors:
Linda Cookson
Bryan Loughrey

LONGMAN
LITERATURE
GUIDES

Longman Literature Guides

Editors: Linda Cookson and Bryan Loughrey

Titles in series:

CONTENTS

PREFACE

Like all professional groups, literary critics have developed their own specialised language. This is not necessarily a bad thing. Sometimes complex concepts can only be described in a terminology far removed from everyday speech. Academic jargon, however, creates an unnecessary barrier between the critic and the intelligent but less practised reader.

This danger is particularly acute where scholarly books and articles are re-packaged for a student audience. Critical anthologies, for example, often contain extracts from longer studies originally written for specialists. Deprived of their original context, these passages can puzzle and at times mislead. The essays in this volume, however, are all specially commissioned, self-contained works, written with the needs of students firmly in mind.

This is not to say that the contributors — all experienced critics and teachers — have in any way attempted to simplify the complexity of the issues with which they deal. On the contrary, they explore the central problems of the text from a variety of critical perspectives, reaching conclusions which are challenging and at times mutually contradictory.

They try, however, to present their arguments in direct, accessible language and to work within the limitations of scope and length which students inevitably face. For this reason, essays are generally rather briefer than is the practice; they address quite specific topics; and, in line with examination requirements, they incorporate precise textual detail into the body of the discussion.

They offer, therefore, working examples of the kind of essay-writing skills which students themselves are expected to develop. Their diversity, however, should act as a reminder that in the field of literary studies there is no such thing as a 'model' answer. Good essays are the outcome of a creative engagement with literature, of sensitive, attentive reading and careful thought. We hope that those contained in this volume will encourage students to return to the most important starting point of all, the text itself, with renewed excitement and the determination to explore more fully their own critical responses.

INTRODUCTION

How to use this volume

Obviously enough, you should start by reading the text in question. The one assumption that all the contributors make is that you are already familiar with this. It would be helpful, of course, to have read further — perhaps other works by the same author or by influential contemporaries. But we don't assume that you have yet had the opportunity to do this and any references to historical background or to other works of literature are explained.

You should, perhaps, have a few things to hand. It is always a good idea to keep a copy of the text nearby when reading critical studies. You will almost certainly want to consult it when checking the context of quotations or pausing to consider the validity of the critic's interpretation. You should also try to have access to a good dictionary, and ideally a copy of a dictionary of literary terms as well. The contributors have tried to avoid jargon and to express themselves clearly and directly. But inevitably there will be occasional words or phrases with which you are unfamiliar. Finally, we would encourage you to make notes, summarising not just the argument of each essay but also your own responses to what you have read. So keep a pencil and notebook at the ready.

Suitably equipped, the best thing to do is simply begin with whichever topic most interests you. We have deliberately organised each volume so that the essays may be read in any order. One consequence of this is that, for the sake of clarity and self-containment, there is occasionally a degree of overlap between essays. But at least you are not forced to follow one — fairly arbitrary — reading sequence.

Each essay is followed by brief 'Afterthoughts', designed to highlight points of critical interest. But remember, these are only there to remind you that it is *your* responsibility to question what you read. The essays printed here are not a series of 'model' answers to be slavishly imitated and in no way should they be regarded as anything other than a guide or stimulus for your own thinking. We hope for a critically involved response: 'That was interesting. But if *I* were tackling the topic . . .!'

Read the essays in this spirit and you'll pick up many of the skills of critical composition in the process. We have, however, tried to provide more explicit advice in 'A practical guide to essay writing'. You may find this helpful, but do not imagine it offers any magic formulas. The quality of your essays ultimately depends on the quality of your engagement with literary texts. We hope this volume spurs you on to read these with greater understanding and to explore your responses in greater depth.

A note on the text

All references are to the New Penguin Shakespeare edition of *Twelfth Night*, ed. M M Mahood.

Kate Flint

*Kate Flint is Fellow and Tutor in
English Literature at Mansfield College,
Oxford. She is the author of numerous
critical works.*

ESSAY

Carnival and cruelty in *Twelfth Night*

Samuel Pepys, writing his diary on 6 January 1663, records: 'To
the Duke's house, and there saw Twelfth-Night acted well,
though it be but a silly play, and not relating at all to the name
or day.' He was mistaken, on more than one count.

Twelfth Night. The last day of Christmas feasting, the last
night of holiday: the day before normal life resumes. Twelfth
Night: a time to put on masks, to play at being who you are not,
to disrupt the normal order of things. A carnival time. Carnival,
according to the Russian critic Mikhail Bakhtin, writing about
the Renaissance in *Rabelais and His World*, was:

> celebrated temporary liberation from the prevailing truth and
> from the established order; it marked the suspension of all
> hierarchical rank, privileges, norms, and prohibitions. Carnival
> was the true feast of time, the feast of becoming, change, and
> renewal.

Shakespeare's play is likewise a suspension in time, but a self-
conscious one, making the reader or spectator aware of the
interplay between festivity and game-playing on the one hand,
and real life on the other. For whilst its plot is both preposterous
and entertaining, its implications are far more serious. Even

while the disguises, the role playing, the gulling and tricking are going on, there's an air of menace, of bullying, which is never far from the surface. Carnival, in other words, can be cruel; can tread on the edge of danger. And this cruelty, the play makes us realise, can be present unrecognised in our daily lives and attitudes as well as in drama, which uses improbabilities and exaggeration to make it visible.

The central game of disguise in *Twelfth Night* is patently improbable. Duke Orsino employs the shipwrecked Viola — dressed up in boy's clothing — to woo the countess Olivia for him. Already, there's potential for comedy, the audience being placed in a position where it knows more than the characters. This position of superior knowledge is reinforced when we learn that Viola's brother Sebastian, whom she's presumed drowned, is still alive. The inevitable happens: Olivia falls in love with Cesario–Viola; and Viola falls in love with Orsino. Falls in love unaccountably, one might think, with someone languishing, love-sick, for another woman, but this is not a play in which we are invited to look below the surface for psychological motiv-ation, even though, in many ways, it's a play about the dangers of being taken in by surfaces. But this dance of courtship takes place against a less frivolous background. Olivia is surrounded by a decidedly off-beat collection of people, forming a foil to the court world presided over by Orsino: Sir Toby Belch's very name gives away his tendency to drink and guzzle; his companion Sir Andrew Aguecheek is decrepit; Malvolio is ludicrous, pompous, ambitious, wordy and vulgar. Feste the jester, like the Fool in *King Lear*, is a very serious fool, who puns on words, contributes a couple of melancholic songs, reminding us that 'Youth's a stuff will not endure' (II.3.50) and generally provides a sardonic commentary on the proceedings. The fool's role was an import-ant one in Shakespearean theatre, forming a bridge between the world of the play and the outside world. Fools were taken seriously: in the spirit of Erasmus's *In Praise of Folly* (1509), they had the licence to utter critical truths; moreover, they were played by actors who were known as entertainers in their own right — in the case of *Twelfth Night*, by Robert Armin. Feste not only has a rapport with the audience as well as with the personages on stage — as we'll see, the play ends with him having the last word — but is also not always immediately on hand when called for, as though, one might say, he's momentarily, disconcertingly, escaped into the 'real' world. His function includes the uttering of generalised comments which bear no specific relation to events taking place on stage, but remind one of the complexities which exist in non-festive existence: 'Anything that's mended is but patched: virtue that transgresses is but patched with sin; and sin that amends is but patched with virtue. If that this simple syllogism will serve, so; if it will not, what remedy?' (I.5.42–46).

To pause on these characters in Olivia's household is to mirror their function within the play: to hold up action, to waste, to ignore, the demands of time. But they do conspire together to produce their own action, in a way which shows up one type of cruelty. Sir Andrew and Sir Toby, together with Maria and Fabian, decide to play a trick on Malvolio, planting a letter which he interprets as being from Olivia, causing him to dress up ludicrously in cross-gartered yellow stockings, and become entangled in cross-purposes. This comedy, however, is continued to the point of sadism as Malvolio ends up imprisoned on the false grounds of madness, further tormented by Feste, in the dark, pretending to be a priest visiting him: mental bullying, which is inadequately summed up by Fabian as 'sportful malice' (V.1.363).

Disguises and misunderstandings, whether deliberate or otherwise, mean that both main and sub-plots are at times hard to follow. But disguises, doubleness, mistaken and blurred identities lead to a more sophisticated type of confusion than that which keeps these plots in motion. They have the function of freeing language from the complete personality of the speaker, so ultimately we end up examining concepts and emotions — concerning the nature of love, loss and grief, or the inherent tendencies within human nature to bullying and violence. They enable violence to be expressed not directly towards individual physical bodies, but metaphorically to the human body in general, through the language used by the players on stage. Whilst the action may lack credibility, the sentiments, unfortunately, do not.

To take two examples: hunting the deer may be a plausible enough aristocratic pastime, and provided the Elizabethans with a familiar enough pun on the organ of feeling and the wild animal. Orsino, however, tells of his infatuation and the torment he experiences in terms which are unusually savage:

> That instant was I turned into a hart,
> And my desires, like fell and cruel hounds,
> E'er since pursue me.

(I.1.22–24)

Right from the beginning, when Viola says that she'll go and serve Orsino, the language suggests not so much playfulness, as an element of violence against her own sexual identity: 'I'll serve this Duke./ Thou shalt present me as an eunuch to him' (I.2.56–57).

Sexuality, the underlying theme of so much of *Twelfth Night*, is, as these two quotations illustrate, frequently described in menacing, predatory terms. Sexual attraction, as a motivating force in the play, is common to all. Even Sir Toby ends up marrying Maria. But it is also an area in which norms, as in carnival, are again turned upside-down. For desire takes, during the action if not the conclusion, little notice of what sex anyone is. Antonio, the sea-captain, follows his master Sebastian around with passionate devotion: 'I could not stay behind you. My desire,/ More sharp than filèd steel, did spur me forth' (III.3.4–5). Sir Andrew Aguecheek has only to see the unfortunate Viola, in the guise of Cesario, talking to Olivia and he challenges him to a duel. At the centre of the story, although Olivia has sworn, in melodramatic fashion enough, that as a form of mourning for her brother, she's going to give up all contact with men:

> . . . like a cloistress she will veilèd walk,
> And water once a day her chamber round
> With eye-offending brine

(I.1.30–32)

she's irrationally smitten on her first meeting with Cesario–Viola — 'Even so quickly may one catch the plague?' (I.5.284). This distribution of emotional energy across the sexes means, of course, that the language of passion becomes detached from the context of who delivers it and to whom. Just as, in the sub-plot, Maria's bawdy jibes match those of Sir Toby Belch and Sir Andrew, so the language of Cesario–Viola's famous wooing speech to Olivia ('Make me a willow cabin at your gate . . .' —

I.5.257ff) moves and persuades in its own right, not because it is delivered by one specific person to another.

Whilst both women and men articulate passionate feelings, the play nonetheless brings into focus the inequality of power in conventionally held attitudes. For the women in this play are notably at the mercy of men's designs, verbal and otherwise. Orsino, throughout, is perhaps the most conspicuously blameworthy in his attitudes. In Act II scene 4, he puts his masculine feelings far above those of womanhood: speaking of his infatuation with Olivia:

> There is no woman's sides
> Can bide the beating of so strong a passion
> As love doth give my heart; no woman's heart
> So big to hold so much, they lack retention.
> Alas, their love may be called appetite,
> No motion of the liver, but the palate
>
> (II.4.92–97)

And, a little later, he begs:

> Make no compare
> Between that love a woman can bear me
> And that I owe Olivia.
>
> (II.4.100–102)

What's more, Orsino drives Viola into articulating the archetypal, Griselda-like pose of passively suffering what the patriarchal order ordains for her: a suppression of feeling which ultimately rots and withers what is natural. She creates an imaginary sister, her double, her real self, to tell both Orsino and the audience of this:

> VIOLA My father had a daughter loved a man —
> As it might be perhaps, were I a woman,
> I should your lordship.
> DUKE   And what's her history?
> VIOLA A blank, my lord. She never told her love,
> But let concealment, like a worm i'the bud,
> Feed on her damask cheek. She pined in thought;
> And with a green and yellow melancholy
> She sat like Patience on a monument,
> Smiling at grief.   (II.4.106–114)

Yet to see the women in the play as victims would be false, despite the violence done to them by some of the language. Viola hardly sits passively, rotting on a monument. Shakespeare uses her as an educator, educating through love. Or rather, it's love itself that does the teaching, for, as I said earlier, it's hard to understand in psychological terms why Viola should be bothered with a duke who sees women in terms of conspicuously offensive clichés:

> . . . women are as roses whose fair flower,
> Being once displayed, doth fall that very hour.
>
> (II.4.38–39)

It is a mark of the strength accorded to Viola in the play that Shakespeare uses her, drawing authority from her borrowed masculine attire, to drive home some educative truths, as she compares the sexes:

> We men may say more, swear more, but indeed
> Our shows are more than will; for still we prove
> Much in our vows, but little in our love.
>
> (II.4.115–117)

Orsino comes to realise this in the final scene of the play, but only after he's uttered some pretty unpleasant sentiments: he seems, almost until the end, more concerned with self-love than with relating sympathetically to another. His pride is horribly hurt when he finds Olivia still does not care for him, even though he has never been given encouragement by her. He threatens first her person: 'Why should I not . . . Kill what I love' (V.1.115–117) (surely not an indication of true love to any Elizabethan remembering another tale of puzzling identities, concerning Solomon, two mothers and a baby) and then Viola–Cesario, whom he is starting to suspect of betraying him. His putative action is directed against three people — the two women and himself:

> . . . this your minion, whom I know you love,
> And whom, by heaven, I swear, I tender dearly,
> Him will I tear out of that cruel eye
> Where he sits crownèd in his master's spite.
> . . .
> I'll sacrifice the lamb that I do love
>
> (V.1.123–128)

He treads dangerously near the language of blasphemy, wishing violence against a higher love.

For a play which, at one level, ends, like a conventional comedy, with the happy pairing off of lovers, the whole of the last scene, in fact, is surprisingly permeated by violence and death. Antonio, the sea-captain who rescued Sebastian, has been arrested and is in danger of his life. The dreadful wrangle between Orsino, Viola and Olivia is broken into by Sir Toby with a 'bloody coxcomb': his head has been damaged, indeed, by Sebastian, who even though he enters justifying his action — an entry which allows the play to move towards its resolution — hardly, therefore, appears as a peaceful saviour. Moreover, his own language is full of physical distress, first expressed towards Antonio: 'How have the hours racked and tortured me/ Since I have lost thee!' (V.1.216–217). Even after the brother and sister have been reunited, and Orsino and Viola's marriage agreed, the angry, baffled, utterly uncomprehending Malvolio reappears, asking:

> Why have you suffered me to be imprisoned,
> Kept in a dark house, visited by the priest,
> And made the most notorious geck and gull
> That e'er invention played on?

(V.1.339–342)

The play does not end with him reconciled with his tormentors on stage: he exits threatening 'I'll be revenged on the whole pack of you!' (V.1.375). Whilst this line in usually delivered for a laugh, it is a perfectly justifiable threat in its own right, given the totally gratuitous torments through which he's been put.

Ultimately, it is the convoluted planning of the plot which ensures that the complications are finally unravelled: obvious artifice, rather than suggesting that solutions are found through the decisions and interventions of individual characters. As Viola says:

> O time, thou must untangle this, not I!
> It is too hard a knot for me t'untie.

(II.2.40–41)

The fact that ultimately forces stronger than individual action help sort things out underlines the play's consoling point that the universe is an ordered one, despite deceptive appearances, and despite the disruptive violence which characterises the emotions of some individuals. From one point of view, it's only accident that stops the socially disruptive implications of one woman marrying another; but from another, it's suggested that there's more than chance at work when Olivia rushes into wedlock with Sebastian: 'you have been mistook./ But nature to her bias drew in that' (V.1.256–257).

Twelfth Night: Epiphany. The play is, among other things, about epiphanies: moments of revelation of identity, of the existence of love — but also showing us its ephemeral nature; its capacity, as an abstract quality, to pass from one person to another. It is about, too, the festive desire to hold back the passage of time, or at least to escape from one's awareness of time passing — although time nonetheless keeps on ticking, as Olivia notes, when, during her wooing of Cesario–Viola, 'the clock upbraids me with the waste of time'. For it is not a play which allows its characters, still less its audience, to remain in that condition of suspended time which constitutes theatrical experience. *Twelfth Night* denies us, too, feelings of completeness at its conclusion. Even the most poignant moment of reconciliation, Viola's reunion with her brother, takes place through conditional language: 'Were you a woman,' says Sebastian, to his sister wearing the boy's clothes in which she androgynously remains until the close:

> Were you a woman, as the rest goes even,
> I should my tears let fall upon your cheek,
> And say, 'Thrice welcome, drownèd Viola.'
>
> (V.1.236–238)

Nor does the play quite close on a conventional re-establishment of gender relations, on the pairs of lovers — Orsino and Viola, Olivia and Sebastian — moving off in harmonious nuptial bliss. The final focus is on the unpartnered figure of Feste. Alone on the stage, he catapults us once again back into the January of the real world:

> When that I was and a little tiny boy,
>   With hey-ho, the wind and the rain;
> A foolish thing was but a toy,
>   For the rain it raineth every day.
>
> (V.1.386–389)

And, in the last stanza of his song, he links the world of the theatre to our own everyday existence, begging the audience for applause as a member of Shakespeare's company, rather than as Feste the Clown:

> A great while ago the world began,
>   With hey-ho, the wind and the rain;
> But that's all one, our play is done,
>   And we'll strive to please you every day.

(V.1.402–405)

His underlying melancholic tone, and the sense of effort which the word 'strive' brings to the acting, further confirm the fact that this is far from being a happy, carefree comedy.

To highlight the more disturbing aspects of the play is, I believe, to return to the Renaissance spirit of carnival: to its knife-edge between the violent and the ridiculous, where the human body itself becomes a figure for spectacle, irrespective of the personality which inhabits it. In conclusion, I draw on Friedrich Nietzsche, the late-nineteenth-century German philosopher, who wrote, in *The Genealogy of Morals* (1887):

> Not so very long ago, a royal wedding or great public celebration would have been incomplete without executions, tortures or *autos-da-fé*; a noble household without some person whose office it was to serve as a butt for everybody's malice and cruel teasing . . . There is no feast without cruelty . . . By way of comfort to the milksops, I would venture the suggestion that in those days pain did not hurt as much.

But this is a vain hope on Nietzsche's part. The fact that not only is there no feast without cruelty, but that the world of carnival, mingling pleasure with pain, merely exaggerates tendencies to be found in real life rather than providing an escape from them, is the sobering lesson which *Twelfth Night* teaches us.

AFTERTHOUGHTS

1

What parallels between the Twelfth Night festival and the play's themes does Flint explore in this essay?

2

Do you agree that *Twelfth Night* is 'not a play in which we are invited to look below the surface for psychological motivation' (page 10)?

3

What do you understand by 'freeing language from the complete personality of the speaker' (page 11)?

4

What forms of violence does Flint identify in this essay?

Cedric Watts

Cedric Watts is Professor of English at Sussex University, and author of many scholarly publications.

ESSAY

The problem of Malvolio

1

The problem concerning Malvolio in *Twelfth Night* has long been recognised but remains difficult. The gist of it is this. Many modern readers or spectators feel that the treatment of Malvolio is distastefully harsh. We expect him to become a butt of humour; we know that in the world of comedy, a rather puritanical and joyless figure is likely to receive comic humiliation; but in this play the humiliation seems severe and protracted. The reader or spectator may thus find that the play as a whole is crucially marred; laughter dies away; a sense of sympathy with the underdog — in this case the duped Malvolio — troubles and complicates the response to the work as a whole. Can it be that Shakespeare is less genially tolerant, less magnanimous in outlook, than he is often supposed to be? Is it perhaps the case that modern audiences are more enlightened than were Shakespeare and his contemporaries? 'He was not of an age, but for all time', claimed Ben Jonson;[1] but are there not occasions when we recognise that Shakespeare, inevitably, was constrained by the

---

[1] Ben Jonson: 'To the Memory of . . . Mr. William Shakespeare', in F E Halliday, *Shakespeare and His Critics* (London, 1958), p. 49.

values of his era, and that time erodes his power and relevance as naturally as the sea erodes a rock?

My discussion has the following plan. In Part 2, I elaborate this problem concerning Malvolio. In Part 3, I consider some counter-arguments. Finally, in Part 4, I attempt to adjudicate.

2

Scholars usually claim that *The Merchant of Venice* was written around 1597, whereas *Twelfth Night* is usually dated 1601, and several comedies (*The Merry Wives of Windsor, Much Ado About Nothing* and *As You Like It*) intervene between them. Nevertheless there are some curious connections between those two plays. In both *The Merchant* and *Twelfth Night* we encounter a character called Antonio who dearly loves a male friend, to whom he lends money, and for whom he imperils his own safety; in both cases, the male friend makes a fortunate marriage to a wealthy lady, and Antonio is eventually delivered from peril. In both plays, a puritanical 'outsider' who is mocked and scorned by others believes, for a while, that he has been granted the power to prevail over his enemies, but they triumph over him, and he is excluded from the final celebrations of love, happiness and good fortune. In *The Merchant of Venice*, that outsider is, of course, Shylock, and in *Twelfth Night* he is Malvolio. Shylock is a much more powerful characterisation, a more grimly ominous figure, and his treatment is more grossly problematic. Malvolio is a slighter character, and his treatment may not be as disturbing; but there are similar problems. In both cases, 'poetic justice' seems unpleasantly ruthless.

What, after all, is Malvolio's offence? We probably think of him as an egoistic kill-joy, for we readily recall the early scene in which he attempts unavailingly to end the noisy and drunken revelry of Sir Toby Belch, Sir Andrew Aguecheek and Feste the Clown:

> My masters, are you mad? Or what are you? Have you no wit,
> manners, nor honesty, but to gabble like tinkers at this time of
> night? Do ye make an ale-house of my lady's house, that ye

squeak out your coziers' catches without any mitigation or remorse of voice? Is there no respect of place, persons, nor time in you?

(II.3.85–91)

The first point to be noted is that his complaint makes very good sense. The late-night revellers in the house of Olivia (who is avowedly mourning her brother's death) are indeed noisy, thoughtless and besotted. Maria, who is no friend to Malvolio, had herself remarked a minute or two previously:

What a caterwauling do you keep here! If my lady have not called up her steward Malvolio and bid him turn you out of doors, never trust me.

(II.3.70–72)

The second point to note is that Malvolio is acting not as an independent person, but as Countess Olivia's dutiful employee, obeying orders:

Sir Toby, I must be round with you. My lady bade me tell you that, though she harbours you as her kinsman, she's nothing allied to your disorders. If you can separate yourself and your misdemeanours, you are welcome to the house. If not, an it would please you to take leave of her, she is very willing to bid you farewell.

(II.3.93–98)

Most of us recall Sir Toby's splendid response: 'Dost thou think, because thou art virtuous, there shall be no more cakes and ale?'; but what we tend to forget is that those words are preceded by Toby's scornfully snobbish remark, 'Art any more than a steward?' Poor Malvolio has to work for his living; he has to obey the orders of a countess, and in this scene he suffers humiliation at the hands of a pair of idle noblemen (one of whom is the countess's cousin) and their associates. It is his unavailing errand at the behest of his employer that provokes Maria, Toby and Andrew to hatch the plot in which Malvolio is duped by the forged letter into the conviction that Olivia loves him; in accordance with the directions in the letter, he enjoys delusions of social promotion, pleasure and power, and dresses and behaves grotesquely; and consequently he is mocked, derided and eventually incarcerated as a madman. Of course, the scene in which he appears as a doting lover, cross-gartered in yellow hose and simpering inanely (III.4), is one of the most joyously farcical scenes in Shakespearian comedy. The protracted torment of Malvolio which follows, however, and which entails the mockery of the incarcerated 'lunatic' by the Clown posing as 'Sir Topas the curate' (IV.2) while Sir Toby and Maria gloat at their victim's wretchedness, is today likely to seem not only unfunny but distasteful: our sympathies move strongly towards Malvolio and against his tormentors. The comedy turns sour. Malvolio has indeed, as he claimed, been 'notoriously abused'; and Olivia evidently concurs: 'He hath been most notoriously abused.' The Duke says, 'Pursue him, and entreat him to a peace'; but nothing in the brief remainder of the text suggests that Malvolio has indeed been placated. His last words in the play, 'I'll be revenged on the whole pack of you!', can credibly be delivered by the actor as the bitter howl of a broken man. Within this predominantly light-hearted, affirmative comedy, there is a jarring, discordant note.

Malvolio does not deserve the destructively relentless mockery which he receives. If he seems a kill-joy, it's chiefly because it's his job to be not only an errand-boy and general manager but also the household policeman — though a power-less and unarmed policeman. If he displays some egoistic vanity in imagining himself to be loved by Olivia, that seems harmless enough; Sir Andrew has similar delusions. Any critic who sug-gests that sympathy for Malvolio is anachronistic, a modern sentimentality alien to the tougher Elizabethan sensibility, is refuted by the text, for (as we noted just now) it is not Malvolio alone but also the perceptive Olivia who regards his humiliation as excessive. Shakespeare evidently felt some qualms about the matter; one sign of this is that we are told that the arrest of the sea-captain who brought Viola to Illyria was made at *Malvolio's* instigation. It looks as though Shakespeare, realising that Mal-volio had simply not been culpable enough to deserve what he received, tardily (and unconvincingly) attempted to reduce the imbalance.

Audiences which enjoy the baiting of Malvolio are not only rather hard-hearted; they are also endorsing the rather snobbish notion that a person who has to work for his living is fair game for idle gentry like Sir Toby and Sir Andrew. Sir Toby's world of 'cakes and ale' may seem appealing; but without stewards like Malvolio, no cakes and ale would be available for the parasitic consumers.

3

That's one argument. Already you can probably sense the form that a counter-argument could take. First, there's the fact that, though Malvolio is acting on Olivia's behalf when he tries to curb the noisy festivities, he is temperamentally joyless and severe in any case: he represents the anti-comic spirit. 'I marvel your ladyship takes delight in such a barren rascal', he says of the Clown; and Olivia aptly replies:

> O, you are sick of self-love, Malvolio, and taste with a distempered appetite. To be generous, guiltless, and of free disposition, is to take those things for bird-bolts that you deem cannon bullets.

(I.5.85–88)

That 'self-love' is amply apparent in Act II scene 5: even before he has found the forged letter, he is fantasising about his marriage to Olivia and the social power this will bring him. If the letter dupes him so completely, that is because it chimes with his egoistic fantasy. Appropriately, he who had once scorned the role of the Clown becomes an unwitting clown himself, voicing coarse puns ('These be her very C's, her U's and her T's; and thus makes she her great P's') and later appearing with an inane grin and in ludicrous attire.

Furthermore, when Malvolio is deluded into thinking he is loved by Olivia, and when later he believes that the Clown is 'Sir Topas', the play is offering yet another demonstration of a capacity for deception and self-deception which seems to make the whole world kin. Orsino initially believes himself to be deeply in love with Olivia, but eventually he will marry Viola, who had previously deceived him so easily in her masculine guise; Olivia, also deceived by that guise, falls in love with 'Cesario' but eventually marries Sebastian, and subsequently mistakes Cesario for her husband; Antonio confuses Cesario with Sebastian, and bitterly reproaches his supposed friend for ingratitude; Sir Andrew challenges Sebastian, thinking he is Cesario; and so forth. The adroitness of the plotting is shown by the way in which the confusions accelerate so markedly towards the denouement. Malvolio, though sane, is mocked by being treated as though he were mad; but this, too, is thematically well integrated, since other characters, confused by disguise, show themselves capable of acting sanely in their own view but crazily in the eyes of others. When Sebastian finds that a stranger (Olivia) is welcoming him lovingly, he remarks:

> What relish is in this? How runs the stream?
> Or I am mad, or else this is a dream.
> Let fancy still my sense in Lethe steep;
> If it be thus to dream, still let me sleep!

(IV.1.59–62)

And later:

> . . . I am ready to distrust mine eyes,
> And wrangle with my reason that persuades me
> To any other trust but that I am mad —
> Or else the lady's mad

(IV.3.13–16)

In short, if Malvolio is fooled, he is one of many dupes in this comic world. As the Duke in *A Midsummer Night's Dream* reminds us, the lunatic and the lover have much in common; and, in *Twelfth Night*, even the noblest figures may be possessed by the benign lunacy of sexual love.

That the mockery of the incarcerated Malvolio seems to be taking a joke too far is clearly recognised in the text. As 'Sir Topas' baits his victim, Sir Toby says:

> I would we were well rid of this knavery. If he may be con-
> veniently delivered, I would he were, for I am now so far in
> offence with my niece that I cannot pursue with any safety this
> sport the upshot.

(IV.2.66–70)

This reflection shows that Shakespeare is fully in command of the play's effects; and readers or spectators who sympathise with Malvolio here are simply responding to the author's own promptings. Why, then, is it that in the concluding scene of clarifications, matches and reconciliations, the author lets Malvolio remain the outsider, an indignant and apparently embittered figure? One irony is that, though Malvolio does not know it, a revenge that might have gratified him has already taken place. Sir Toby's scheme to trick Cesario and Sir Andrew into fighting a duel has resulted in 'a bloody coxcomb' for Toby (and a broken head for Andrew), inflicted by Sebastian; so the biters have been bitten in their turn. Maria, who had conceived the plan to trick Malvolio, is finally married to Toby, which (in view of her spouse's character) may be regarded as both reward and punishment. So indeed, 'the whirligig of time brings in his revenges'.

Nevertheless, Malvolio leaves the stage with his cry, 'I'll be revenged on the whole pack of you!': he leaves as an apparently vindictive and unreconciled figure. Much depends on the voicing and the staging here. He could, as when the role was played by Laurence Olivier, sound like a crazed and venomous outcast; but other actors have made him sound merely petulantly self-pitying, and thus have made the proposed reconciliation ('Pursue him, and entreat him to a peace') appear altogether more hopefully plausible. After all, the Duke says that the nuptial celebrations are dependent on Malvolio's supplying information about the missing captain. Even if Malvolio's exit seems to add a dash of sourness to the prevailing sweetness of the close, such effects are not unexpected in Shakespearian drama. Near the end of *Love's Labour's Lost*, a messenger brings news of death, and 'the scene begins to cloud'. In *Antony and Cleopatra*, a clown enters with bawdy banter just as Cleopatra prepares her regal suicide; so, if Shakespeare can there offer a counterpoint of tragic and comic, why should we not accept that in an otherwise harmonious close to *Twelfth Night* there may be an astringent element of bitterness? A similar desire for an astringent contrast seems to result in the song by Feste which provides the coda to the play: the melody is predominantly melancholy, and, though the wording is so idiotically obscure as to make commentators attempt painful mental acrobatics, the refrain 'For the rain it raineth every day' is unequivocally pessimistic.

4

Section 2 had argued that something goes wrong in the play: the treatment of Malvolio is finally unsatisfactory, as though Shakespeare were not fully in control of matters. Section 3 argued that Shakespeare's imagination knows what it's doing, and that Malvolio's humiliation is appropriately or sufficiently integrated with the surrounding comic action. Critical uneasiness about the character is evident from the amount of space that he receives in commentators' discussions of the work. What is problematic for commentators, however, may be a golden opportunity for directors and actors; sometimes they may prefer to amplify discord, sometimes they may amplify harmony: the text offers room for manoeuvre. In this play, Malvolio is the character with most 'play' — with most flexibility for theatrical expression and interpretation. Stage histories cite Malvolios who have been variously grave and dignified, vacuous and fantastic, old kill-joys and young upstarts. Thus, Malvolio's revenge has been accomplished, in the sense that he has evidently become the main centre of interest and attention: any great actor would rather choose that role than Orsino's or Sebastian's. There's another revenge to be borne in mind, too. We are told that Malvolio is 'a kind of puritan'; and in 1649 his fellow-puritans, having gained power in England, executed King Charles I. Perhaps the triumphant Parliamentarians included some vengeful stewards.

AFTERTHOUGHTS

1

How would you choose to stage Malvolio's final exit (page 25)? See also the comments of Alexander (pages 88–89).

2

Do you find Feste's final song 'idiotically obscure' (page 25)? See also the comments of Holderness (pages 103–105).

3

If Shakespeare's text offers 'room for manoeuvre' (page 26), can there be such a thing as a correct interpretation of *Twelfth Night*?

4

How effective a resolution to the 'problem' of Malvolio do you find Watts's concluding paragraph (page 26)?

John Saunders

John Saunders is Lecturer in English Literature at the West Sussex Institute of Higher Education, and Awarder in English Literature A level for the Oxford and Cambridge Schools Examinations Board.

ESSAY

'What's in a name?': games with names in *Twelfth Night*

Play in a variety of forms was integral to the festivity associated with the Elizabethan celebration of Twelfth Night. In this essay I shall begin by looking at the word-games connected with some of the more important names in Shakespeare's play. I shall then move on to consider the part played by names in creating and developing dramatic situations.

The play on names begins in the second scene of *Twelfth Night* when the audience learn that the setting is 'Illyria'. In no other play by Shakespeare is the name of the place in which the action occurs so consciously or so mysteriously foregrounded:

> VIOLA   What country, friends, is this?
> CAPTAIN   This is Illyria, lady.
> VIOLA   And what should I do in Illyria?
>   My brother he is in Elysium.

(I.2.1–4)

Viola's pairing of 'Illyria' and 'Elysium' draws attention to both similarities and differences between the two names. Though similar in sound, Elysium is in some ways the antithesis of Illyria. In Greek mythology Elysium was the resting place of the happy dead, a kind of heaven; in *Twelfth Night* Illyria is — initially, at least — the place of the unhappy living. However, like Elysium, Illyria is an exotic-sounding name, suggesting that it is no ordinary place. (It was, in fact, the Elizabethan name for what we now call Yugoslavia.) It may just be a lucky chance that taken together Illyria and Elysium suggest a third word, 'delirium', which might be defined as 'an excited state of mind, bordering on madness'.[1] We have already experienced something of Orsino's derangement in the first scene, and he is not the only sufferer. In Illyria love, for all characters, is a form of madness. 'Are all the people mad?' (IV.1.26) Sebastian asks on being mistaken for Cesario. Moments later he has fallen in love with Olivia who inspires in him the following meditation:

> What relish is in this? How runs the stream?
> Or I am mad, or else this is a dream.
> Let fancy still my sense in Lethe steep;
> If it be thus to dream, still let me sleep!

(IV.1.59–63)

Here the reference to Lethe, the mythological river of forgetfulness, may help to reinforce Illyria's link with Elysium, suggesting that it has become, or is becoming, a kind of heaven.

The conscious foregrounding of names continues in scene 2 as Viola asks the Captain, 'Who governs here?' (I.2.24). The Captain tells her it is Orsino:

> A noble Duke, in nature as in name.

(I.2.25)

There is evidence to suggest that a real duke named Orsino may have been the guest of honour at the first ever performance of *Twelfth Night* and it has been argued that Shakespeare chose to call his fictional duke 'Orsino' as a compliment to this distinguished visitor. However, the name Orsino is appropriate in

---

[1] According to the *Oxford English Dictionary*, the first recorded usage of the word 'delirium' dates from 1599. It is generally agreed that Shakespeare wrote *Twelfth Night* in 1601.

other ways. Translated literally, it means 'little bear'. Bears in Elizabethan England were renowned for their savagery and their ravenous appetites. We will later have a glimpse of Orsino's 'savage jealousy' (V.1.117) when he threatens to kill Viola. We have already heard him speak of his hunger:

> If music be the food of love, play on,
> Give me excess of it, that, surfeiting,
> The appetite may sicken, and so die.

> (I.1.1–3)

A 'noble Duke', Orsino yearns to feed on 'music', 'the food of love'. Olivia has spurned him. But Viola is preparing to serve him as 'an eunuch' (I.2.57) and in so doing will answer his call for music:

> . . . for I can sing
> And speak to him in many sorts of music

> (I.2.58–59)

In Shakespeare's mind there must have been a strong association between bears and music, an association which was made more directly when he came to write *Othello*. In one of this play's most poignant moments, Othello, tricked into believing that his wife is an adultress, remembers her as: 'an admirable musician' who can 'sing the savageness out of a bear' (IV.1.184–185). Perhaps this idea of music's power over bears may have influenced Shakespeare in his choice of the names for both Orsino and Viola.

Viola's name has clear musical connotations and her musical significance is indirectly reinforced when the Captain compares Sebastian (the twin brother whose role she is about to assume) to 'Arion' (I.2.15), a mythological figure who had been saved from drowning by a dolphin charmed by his music. It may have been Shakespeare's original intention to accentuate Viola's musical significance even further by having her join the court as a practising musician, both singing and playing to Orsino. As the text stands we do not hear Viola sing and she is certainly not cast as a eunuch. However, we do experience her speaking to Orsino in a particularly lyrical form of blank verse, a 'sort' of music. The most important scene is Act II scene 4, where she in effect woos the Duke. In this scene, Orsino's opening words:

> Give me some music

initiate the form and mood of the interchange which follows. The scene is divided into three sections. In the first, Orsino and Viola listen to a piece of music and talk lyrically of love, Viola hinting that she loves someone older than herself. The section ends with a pair of couplets which demonstrate the harmony developing between them (the nearness of their rhyming further emphasising their closeness at this moment):

> ORSINO For women are as roses, whose fair flower,
>   Being once displayed, doth fall that very hour.
> VIOLA And so they are. Alas, that they are so,
>   To die, even when they to perfection grow.
>
> (II.4.38–41)

Their duet is interrupted by the arrival of Feste, the singing of his song and his mocking, prosaic exit. In the third section of the scene the poetic duet between Orsino and Viola continues. He 'sings' of his love for Olivia in somewhat lofty, strident abstractions, bordering on cliché:

> There is no woman's sides
> Can bide the beating of so strong a passion
> As love doth give my heart
>
> (II.4.92–94)

In her answer, Viola indirectly 'sings' of her love for Orsino by telling him of the imaginary sister who, like herself, was unable to express her love:

> She never told her love,
>   But let concealment, like a worm i'the bud,
>   Fced on her damask cheek. She pined in thought,
>   And with a green and yellow melancholy,
>   She sat like Patience on a monument,
>   Smiling at grief. Was not this love indeed?
>
> (II.4.109–114)

In this speech, Viola's concrete, poetic image highlights the emptiness of Orsino's more grandiloquent language and in so doing suggests the shallowness of the feelings he has expressed. However, though Orsino is deeply moved by Viola's 'fiction', the scene ends with him resolving to continue with his wooing of Olivia.

Act II scene 4 is important in establishing the depth of the relationship between Viola and Orsino and, in so doing, preparing for the concordant ending when in the play's final scene Orsino discovers that it is Viola and not Olivia whom he loves. In musical terms, this final concord brings to a harmonious resolution a discord which has been dominant from the opening scene, where we first learn of the hopelessness of Orsino's passion for Olivia. There are clear similarities between Olivia and Viola. Both are young women of noble birth who have recently lost their fathers. At the start of the play, both seem to have lost their brothers. It is, surely, not accidental that the two have names which are similar in sound and spelling. If only at a subconscious level, we all must experience the name OLIVIA as a near anagram or discordant variant of VIOLA. This might at first seem an outlandish idea, but a similar kind of play on words is integral to the play's sub-plot, where Maria traps MALVOLIO by means of a letter which refers to:

M.O.A.I.

Malvolio on discovering that 'every one of these letters are in my name' (II.5.137), infers that he is the object of his mistress's passion. (Had the letters been:

V.O.A.I.

they would have been an anagramatic clue which might have lead to any of three solutions: MALVOLIO, VIOLA, OLIVIA.)

Much play has been made on Malvolio's name, which has been taken to mean 'ill wisher', 'bad appetite', 'evil will' and 'I love Mall'. For my purposes, I will argue that the name, like Olivia's, plays on Viola's and that (again if only at a subconscious level) it suggests something like 'evil music', preparing us for Malvolio's final discordant exit: 'I'll be revenged on the whole pack of you!' (V.1.375). In name and nature, Malvolio is an enemy of festivity and, as such, an enemy of the spirit of the Twelfth Night season. Leader of the pack of revellers against him is Sir Toby Belch who, in the scene of midnight revelry (II.3), most memorably expresses the conflict between life-denying virtue and life-affirming indulgence when he asks

Malvolio: 'Dost thou think, because thou art virtuous, there shall be no more cakes and ale?' (II.3.111–112).

The Captain might well have said of Sir Toby, 'a flatulent knight, in nature as in name'. Sir Toby's response to the arrival of Viola in Olivia's court — 'A plague o'these pickle-herring!' (I.5.115–116) — ensures that in *Twelfth Night* the idea of 'appetite' is not confined to idealistic love. But, as his name clearly indicates, his indulgence is habitual, not just confined to seasonal celebrations. Sir Toby's name should presumably also be a guide to his appearance. It would be a bold director who chose to play him as tall and elegantly refined. The other revellers also have significant names. The relationship between Sir Andrew's name and nature is equally straightforward. Though there have been several games with one or more of his names (it being ingeniously suggested that the name Andrew closely echoes the Spanish word *andrajo*, 'a despicable rogue', while Aguecheek plays on the Spanish *aguicia cica*, meaning 'little wit'), most obviously the name Aguecheek suggests the facial quivering of a coward easily moved to terror. There might, however, be some advantages in playing Sir Andrew as outwardly robust, 'a great eater of beef' (I.3.82), who has devoted his youth to 'fencing, dancing, and bear-baiting' (I.3.90), an interpretation which would make Viola's terror in the duel scene a little more credible.

For Feste, the fool, the third of the revellers confronted by Malvolio, there is no congruence between name and character. Feste's name reveals his function and — depending on the director — might dictate his costume, but it does not reveal his nature. First, he is only superficially festive. Though he plays a part in the scene of midnight misrule, for much of the action he is an outsider, unmoved by the season of indulgence and gazing unerringly at the weaknesses and deceptions of those around him. He takes no part in the relatively innocent gulling of Malvolio but later, in the role of Sir Topas (topaz is a stone which was thought to cure madness) he torments Malvolio cruelly, threatening the play's festive mood. Moreover, the songs Feste sings are far from festive. The first stanza of 'O mistress mine' is not inappropriate in its indirect commentary on the transformation taking place within Olivia, whose 'true love' is about to arrive, but the second stanza turns to the inevitability of time's passing, concluding that: 'Youth's a stuff will not

B

endure' (II.3.50). The conclusion goes counter to the mood of the moment. We sense that, in spite of Sir Toby's flirtation with Maria and Sir Andrew's claim to have been 'adored once' (II.3.174), love and youth have bypassed both of them. Similarly, the song which Feste sings to Orsino, 'Come away [meaning *hurry to me*], death', may suit Orsino's indulgent, melancholy mood, but is hardly appropriate in a play about festivity — its imagery of yew and cypress trees, of shrouds, corpses and graves, celebrating death rather than love. In Shakespeare's mind the associations between the fool and death had recently been expressed through the skull in *Hamlet* which turns out to be that of Yorick, the court jester. And Feste's final song with its refrain, 'For the rain it raineth every day', provides a conclusion for *Twelfth Night* which ensures that we all know that by the end of the play the festivities are over and we have to contend once again with winter. (An echo of the song is heard in *King Lear*.)

Though he is named as Feste only once (II.4.11), Feste is repeatedly called 'fool'. However, his function in a world where 'Foolery . . . shines everywhere' (III.1.37–38) is not to play the fool but to reveal the folly in others. Throughout the play the mantle of fool is taken on at various times by many of the other characters. Sometimes a character is named 'fool', as when Feste 'proves' to Olivia that she, not he, warrants the title: 'Take away the fool, gentlemen' (I.5.66–67). Sometimes the folly is implicit but unnamed, as when Feste mocks Orsino's mind as 'a very opal' (II.4.74). Central to the shifting role of fool is the continual gullery. Sir Andrew, 'a foolish knight' (I.3.14) who acknowledges that many do call him 'fool' (II.5.80) is the play's leading gull, trapped by Sir Toby into revealing his foolishness as suitor, wit and duellist. Viola, in the mock duel scene has her moment of folly, another of Sir Toby's victims. The central episode of gullery, once discovered, earns Malvolio the tender accolade, 'poor fool' (V.1.367) from his mistress, Olivia. But, perhaps the play's most absolute fool is not Sir Andrew or Malvolio but the worldy-wise, manipulator, Sir Toby. In the final scene, we discover that Sir Toby has married the marriage-hungry Maria as a reward for her duping of Malvolio. Feste earlier suggests that 'fools are as like husbands as pilchers are to herrings', the husband being 'the bigger' (III.1.32–33).

Feste is by nature neither festive nor a fool. He describes

himself to Viola (disguised, of course, as Cesario) as Olivia's 'corrupter of words' (III.1.34–35). This revelation comes in an important but often overlooked exchange at the start of Act III, where Feste and Viola begin to explore the limitations and elusiveness of language. It is a witty exchange which requires a modern reader to make constant forays to the notes or glossary, and as such it is often glossed over. It is, however, integral to the subject of this essay, since it highlights some similarities between words and names.

The exchange begins with one of the few verbal jokes in the play which probably even Sir Andrew would have understood:

> VIOLA Dost thou live by thy tabor?
> FESTE No, sir, I live by the church.

> (III.1.1–3)

Discovering that Viola is adept at word-games, Feste starts playing more seriously. He mocks the age in which they live as one where:

> A sentence is but a cheveril glove to a good wit; how quickly the wrong side may be turned outward!

> (III.1.11–13)

By now the audience will have encountered enough of Sir Toby's word-games — 'let her except, before excepted' (I.3.6), 'Confine! I'll confine myself no finer than I am' (I.3.9) — to know what Feste means. Viola's playful answer:

> They that dally nicely with words may quickly make them wanton

> (III.1.14–15)

introduces a new dimension into the game. She means that ingenious word-play can render language ambiguous, but Feste responds to the sexual connotations in 'dally' and 'wanton', and proceeds to link words with names and to provide his reasons: 'I would therefore my sister had had no name, sir' (III.1.16) for 'her name's a word, and to dally with that word might make my sister wanton' (III.1.18–19) for 'words are very rascals, since bonds disgraced them' (III.1.19–20). Here, for a moment, the play's language foregrounds the relationship between words and names and the things and people to which they refer. In modern linguistic terminology, a word or a name is called a 'signifier' and the thing or person to which it refers is called the 'signified'. As a 'corrupter of words', Feste continually breaks the intended bond between signifier and signified — ('No, sir, I live by the church' is an obvious example, Viola having intended the signifiers 'live by' to signify the activity of earning a living). However, when it comes to names rather than words, both Feste and Viola *represent* — in different ways — the corruption of bonds. Feste the fool is neither festive nor a fool. And his companion on stage is neither Cesario nor a man. In choosing to take on the role of Cesario, Viola has dallied with her name, has broken the bond between herself and it, and has unwittingly become 'wanton'. She, Sebastian's sister, has taken on his appearance and has moved Olivia sexually. 'Disguise, I see thou art a wickedness' (II.2.27), Viola says on discovering that Olivia has fallen in love with her, the words foreshadowing Feste's comments on the corruption of language.

In his exchange with Viola, Feste (anticipating modern linguistic philosophy) touches on one of the problems of attempting to use language to talk about language. In explaining why he cannot provide a reason to explain why 'bonds' have 'disgraced words', he says:

> Troth, sir, I can yield you none without words, and words are grown so false, I am loath to prove reason with them.
>
> (III.1.22–24)

The difficulty of using language to discuss language is accentuated when talking about a play. As readers of *Twelfth Night* we know that the name Viola signifies the imaginary heroine of the play. However, in a performance of *Twelfth Night*, there is a second signifier, the member of the cast who plays the role of Viola. When Viola disgraces the bond between herself and her name by taking on the role of Cesario and donning a male costume (another kind of signifier), the link between signifiers and signified becomes even more complex. Let us for a moment resort to an algebraic notation and refer to the person who plays Viola as X when in a female costume and as Y when in the role and garb of Cesario. Let's refer to the person playing Sebastian as Z. To the audience both X and Y signify Viola. However, to the inhabitants of Illyria Y and Z seem identical. Olivia loses her heart to Y, assuming Y is Z, marries Z and is mortified by Y's reluctance to accept the marriage bond. Orsino is moved almost to murder through his inability to distinguish Y from Z; Antonio is moved near to suicide through the same confusion. I have used the neutral term 'person' to allow for both Elizabethan and modern productions. As conceived by Shakespeare, the relationships between signifier and signified become even more complex when discussing the role of Viola. Viola would have been played by a boy. X would have signified a false femininity for the play's audience who knew that all female roles were taken by males. Y would have signified a false masculinity to the inhabitants of Illyria, but for the audience this fictional falsity would have moved Y closer to his true sexuality.

Other comic situations within the play stem from confusions between signifiers and signifieds. Sir Andrew Aguecheek is presented to Viola by Sir Toby as an assailant who is 'quick, skilful, and deadly' (III.4.221) and as 'a devil in private brawl' (III.4.231–232). Sir Toby and the audience know that Sir Andrew (as his name signifies) has less 'blood in his liver' than 'will clog the foot of a flea' (III.2.59–60). Sir Toby assumes (rightly) that Viola (or Cesario) is similarly lacking in valour. However, Sir Toby becomes the victim of his own joke when he too fails to distinguish between Y and Z. But it is the sub-plot which deals with the gulling of Malvolio that provides the most notable comedy relating to names. Malvolio (let's call him M.A.I.O.) wrongly assumes that the signifier M.O.A.I. signifies himself. M.O.A.I. is as we know a fictional construct of Maria's. M.A.I.O. attempts to become the M.O.A.I. as signified in Maria's letter. At the start of the play Malvolio is in nature, in name and in outward appearance a puritan and an enemy to festivity. He signifies this through his dress and his manner, wearing black and never smiling. In attempting to become M.O.A.I., the assumed object of Olivia's love, he is required to smile and to dress extravagantly in cross-gartered yellow stockings. M.A.I.O. becomes M.O.A.I. and, though wanting to signify that he is a lover, is classified as a madman.

The play's name, *Twelfth Night*, signifies that it will be a comedy concerned with seasonal festivity. However, the season of Twelfth Night had gained its significance partly from religious ritual. In the religious calendar, Twelfth Night was the time of the Epiphany, when the showing forth of the true, *kingly* nature of the Christ-child was celebrated. Some commentators have argued that the name Cesario (which through its derivation from Caesar signifies kingship) becomes religiously significant in the play's final Act when Viola reveals her true self. Whether or not we accept this religious dimension, the idea of 'epiphany' is integral to the play's ending, the play's final scene consisting of a series of revelations, where signifiers and signifieds are publicly reconciled. For Orsino, the discovery of Viola's name and nature should come as a triple epiphany, he learning in an instant that his Cesario is a woman, that he loves her and that her name is Viola. For most modern audiences — already familiar with the play — there is no moment of discovery in the name. However, the original audience, not having had programmes or cast lists, would not have known or heard Viola's name until the closing moments of the play. Here, when Viola's identity is at last revealed, the name sounds three times in a dozen lines, culminating in Viola's declaration:

That I am Viola

(V.1.250)

Only at this moment, as signifier and signified come together for the first time, is Orsino's call for music finally answered.

AFTERTHOUGHTS

1

How convincing do you find Saunders's suggestions about the appropriateness of individual characters' names (pages 29–34)?

2

Would you agree that Sir Toby's marriage to Maria makes him 'the play's most absolute fool' (page 34)? Compare Saunders's interpretation with that of Watts (page 25).

3

Explain the relevance to Saunders's argument of his exploration of the relationship between 'signifier' and 'signified' (pages 35–38).

4

Compare Saunders's comments on Epiphany (pages 37–38) with Flint's (pages 16–17).

David Lewis

David Lewis is Director of English Studies at Barton Peveril College, Hampshire. He is a Chief Examiner for AS-level English.

ESSAY

Deception in *Twelfth Night*

All drama is basically deception, an illusion in which actors pretend to be somebody else, aided by the audience's 'suspension of disbelief', as Coleridge put it, but many plays use deception as a major ingredient in their construction. We might expect a play from around 1601 with the title *Twelfth Night* to reflect something of the court masques and revels popular at the time, in which an essential element was disguise. It is interesting that an Italian comedy which Shakespeare almostly certainly knew and from which he may have taken some ideas for *Twelfth Night* was entitled *Gl'Ingannati* — 'The Deceived Ones'. Another possible source was *Gl'Inganni* — 'The Deceptions' — arguably a more appropriate title than 'Twelfth Night', and certainly a better subtitle than 'What You Will', for the whole play is constructed as a complex tapestry of cleverly interwoven deceptions. Almost all the characters in the play are engaged either in deceiving themselves or in deliberately or accidentally deceiving others.

The play begins with a striking example of self-deception, initially amusing for the audience, in Orsino's conviction that he loves Olivia. He doesn't catch even a glimpse of her in the three months' course of the play until the final scene. Instead he woos by proxy and is presented as the conventional love-sick lover, luxuriating in the paradoxically 'sweet pangs' (II.4.16) of melancholia. In two scenes he looks for music to relieve his passion, but seems insincere in wanting it to lessen his appetite for love, for he enjoys his suffering intensely. He easily convinces himself that he can identify with the betrayed lover in Feste's song, enjoying all the associations of melancholy — the 'sad cypress', the 'poor corpse', the 'sad true lover' (II.4.50–65). He claims to be the model of the true lover, 'unstaid and skittish' (II.4.18) in everything except constancy to the beloved. Clearly Orsino has retreated into a world of imagination and unreality, indulging in conceited language:

> So full of shapes is fancy
> That it alone is high fantastical.

> (I.1.14–15)

Orsino's sense of superiority ('my love, more noble than the world' — II.4.80) leads him to the totally unjustified assumption that he has a 'true place' in Olivia's favour (V.1.121) and that he will rule her as her 'king' (I.1.40). His understanding of women is absurdly false:

> There is no woman's sides
> Can bide the beating of so strong a passion
> As love doth give my heart

> (II.4.92–94)

Viola punctures this pretentiousness when she argues that women's love is as deep-seated and true as men's. The Duke's genuine concern for Cesario's 'sister' suggests that behind all the false affectation there is a real person struggling to get out. His self-deception remains, however, until very near the end of the play, for in the final scene when he at last sees Olivia face to face he addresses her with typically preposterous posturing:

> You uncivil lady,
> To whose ingrate and unauspicious altars
> My soul the faithfull'st offerings have breathed out
> That e'er devotion tendered!

> (V.1.110–113)

In his self-deception Orsino has remained a completely static character, but there has been a development of real emotion centring on Cesario, so that when he discovers that Cesario is actually a woman he can allow the reality to sweep aside the self-deception and admit the falseness of his supposed love for Olivia. It is this that makes credible the otherwise extremely sudden switch from Olivia to Viola, and indeed saves the Duke from being merely an effete insipid buffoon. We can see him finally as a fit husband for Viola.

Just as Orsino's self-deception is produced by inexperience of real love or the real world, so is that of Olivia. If we see her as an extremely intelligent, sensitive and lively eighteen-year-old then she is mistakenly deceiving herself into thinking that it is not only right and proper to mourn for her brother for seven years and abjure the company and sight of men, but that she has a suitable temperament to see it through. This deception is very quickly dispelled when she shows an inordinate interest in the young man at her gates in Act I scene 5 and is sufficiently intrigued to invite him in and then fall head over heels in love. It is interesting to note that her love-sickness, produced by the deception practised on her unwittingly by Viola, parallels the Duke's. She uses the word 'sad' three times in just a few lines early in Act III scene 4, and Viola in the same scene observes:

> With the same 'haviour that your passion bears
> Goes on my master's griefs.

(III.4.202–203)

For both Orsino and Olivia self-deception serves as an avoidance of the real world and of real emotions. As soon as they acknowledge reality, they cease to delude themselves. Some other characters, however, never do emerge from their self-deception.

In the sub-plot, the most notable example of a self-deceiver is of course Malvolio. His sense of superiority is greater even than Orsino's. He sees himself as surrounded by 'idle, shallow things', not of his 'element' (III.4.122–123) and this encourages his ambition to become inflated to the point where he considers that a marriage to Olivia is entirely appropriate. He can even believe that Olivia loves him — 'Maria once told me she [Olivia] did affect me' (II.5.23–24) (surely an example of a mischievous lie by Maria?). He is not in love with Olivia for herself, but he very much fancies the status, the power and the opulent life-style that this marriage could confer. In the box-hedge scene he pictures himself sitting in state in a velvet gown, playing with a rich jewel, with seven servants jumping to obey his slightest command. The absurdity of this notion does not lie principally in Malvolio's humble status, for he is referred to throughout as a 'gentleman', and, as he points out, 'the Lady of the Strachy married the yeoman of the wardrobe' (II.5.38–39). Moreover, Olivia has a high regard for him, which suggests that his ambitions are not totally absurd: in the 'smiling' scene, even though she thinks Malvolio is mad, Olivia can still say: 'Let some of my people have a special care of him. I would not have him miscarry for the half of my dowry' (III.4.62–64). Maria supports this later in the scene: 'My lady would not lose him, for more than I'll say' (lines 104–105). Malvolio is conscious of this high regard: 'she uses me with a more exalted respect than anyone else that follows her' (II.5.26–27). But he cannot see how his personal qualities make it impossible for Olivia ever to consider him as a husband. She is well aware of his inflated ego: 'you are sick of self-love, Malvolio' (I.5.85). Sir Toby sees him as 'an overweening rogue' (II.5.29), and Maria, with her customary perception, describes him as:

> an affectioned ass . . . the best persuaded of himself, so crammed, as he thinks, with excellencies, that it is his grounds of faith that all that look on him love him
>
> (II.3.141–45)

This lack of self-criticism or self-awareness makes him utterly vulnerable to Maria's subsequent plan to ridicule him.

If Malvolio's self-deception is amusing but objectionable, that of Sir Andrew is more purely comic. In many ways he mirrors Malvolio's inflated view of himself, but he constantly puts himself down too, so that there is something rather pathetic about his self-delusion, as if it is an attempt to bolster his basic timidity and lack of confidence. He claims to have spent his time in 'fencing, dancing, and bear-baiting' (I.3.90), and that his leg is 'strong' for dancing (I.3.127), yet his skill in fencing is nonexist-ent as the comic duel later shows, and his dancing is ludicrous, though hugely amusing to Sir Toby. The macho reference to bear-baiting is echoed in Sir Andrew's protestations 'I care not for good life' (II.3.36), and 'let me alone for swearing' (III.4.180), but these serve only to conjure up an absurd picture of Sir Andrew as the would-be roguish roisterer.

Like Malvolio, only even more ludicrously, Sir Andrew also sees himself as a husband for Olivia, but this deception is deliberately fostered by Sir Toby, who ostensibly has 'brought [him] in one night here, to be her wooer' (I.3.15), but in reality as a source of entertainment and money for himself. Sir Andrew is persuaded that the money is vital for a successful outcome: 'Thou hadst need send for more money . . . If thou hast her not i'the end, call me cut' (II.3.175–180), but in fact Sir Toby pockets it himself. As he confides to Fabian, 'I have been dear to him, lad, some two thousand strong or so' (III.2.52–53) — a sum which represents two-thirds of Sir Andrew's annual income. This exploitation is remarkably similar to that of Roderigo by Iago in the later play *Othello*, but whereas Iago is unquestionably a villain, audiences normally find Sir Toby a genial and sympathetic rogue, though if we examine his heartlessness towards Sir Andrew he is far less appealing. He expresses his real opinion vividly to Fabian: 'For Andrew, if he were opened and you find so much blood in his liver as will clog the foot of a flea, I'll eat the rest of the anatomy' (III.2.58–60). And in the final scene, when Sir Andrew offers to help him in his wounded state, Sir Toby attacks him spitefully: 'Will you help? An asshead, and a coxcomb, and a knave — a thin-faced knave, a gull!' (V.1.203–204). These accusations may be accurate, but to utter them is cruel. Sir Toby uses deception in the form of flattery in Sir Andrew's presence, praising, for example, his inept dancing, and in his absence he frequently uses irony, here a form of comic deception. The best example of this is in an early scene with Maria, where, for their mutual amusement, Sir Toby utters extravagant praise of Sir Andrew, while clearly not believing a word of it, referring to his playing the viol-de-gamboys, speaking three or four languages fluently, and having 'all the good gifts of nature' (I.3.25).

The most amusing example of deception practised on Sir Andrew is the challenge to, and subsequent duel with, Cesario. Sir Toby seizes on Sir Andrew's natural inclination to be 'a great' (if cowardly) 'quarreller', (I.3.27), already exhibited in his absurd notion of challenging Malvolio, and making a fool of him by failing to appear (II.3). Sir Toby was eager then to write or deliver the challenge, but he sees a more promising opportunity when Sir Andrew is affronted by the favours which he has seen Olivia pay to Cesario. It could be suggested that Sir Toby is motivated by a desire to maintain his own source of income by boosting Sir Andrew's flagging confidence as a suitor, but the chief concern seems to be merely to provide entertainment, which it certainly does. At first Sir Toby is not optimistic but he throws himself into the deception with tremendous zest, abetted by Fabian, and they successfully flatter Sir Andrew by extravagantly approving his pathetic written challenge. Sir Toby's invention reaches a peak as the deception is extended to Cesario and each duellist in turn is reduced to jelly with accounts of the other's fury and skill — of Sir Andrew's having killed three men in private quarrels, and of Cesario's being fencer to the Shah. Sir Toby eventually overstretches himself when he persuades Sir Andrew to have another go at the apparently cowardly Cesario, and is himself deceived into being thrashed by Sebastian. The other comic highlight of *Twelfth Night* is developed, interestingly, over exactly the same stretch of the play — both plots begin in Act II scene 3, and both continue into the final scene — and in the same way is based on deception, but whereas the tricking of Sir Andrew was almost entirely Sir Toby's doing, the deception of Malvolio is the brain-child of Maria, the 'noble gull-catcher' (II.5.180). Her plan is utterly successful because it exploits Malvolio's self-delusion. She plays on his vanity — the physical attractions of his beard, leg, gait, eye, forehead and complexion — and by a master-stroke includes several references to Fortune: 'Thy fates open their hands' (II.5.141) . . . 'worthy to touch Fortune's fingers' (lines 151–152). Just before he found the letter Malvolio declared his belief that ''Tis but fortune, all is fortune' (line 23). The letter serves to confirm his conviction that his destiny is in the hands of a benevolent deity — 'Jove and my stars be praised' (lines 165–166). Even Maria is amazed that anyone in his right mind could have believed 'such impossible passages of grossness' (III.2.68), for Malvolio has obeyed 'every point of the letter that I dropped to betray him' (lines 73–74).

The deception is total, as Sir Toby points out:

. . . thou hast put him in such a dream, that when the image of it
leaves him, he must run mad.

(II.5.186–187)

Malvolio must surely be under the influence of this 'dream'
when he declares that Olivia *did* commend his yellow stockings
and praise his cross-gartering, for her genuine horror at his
appearance in Act III scene 4 belies this. The brilliant humour of
the early part of this scene derives from Malvolio's complete self-
deception, as he sees encouragement in Olivia's 'Wilt thou go to
bed, Malvolio?' (line 28), in her use of the word 'fellow', and in
her sending Sir Toby so that he can practise being stubborn to
him. Nothing could be further from the truth than Malvolio's
belief that he has 'limed' Olivia and that 'nothing that can be,
can come between me and the full prospect of my hopes' (lines
81–82). Indeed, 'His very genius hath taken the infection of the
device' (lines 128–129).

If we have felt largely contempt for Malvolio so far, it is
surely at this point that we begin to feel some pity too. When
Malvolio declares 'Jove, not I, is the doer of this, and he is to be
thanked' (lines 82–83) we can see here either an absurd assumption that the Almighty is preoccupied with his fortunes, or
possibly that Malvolio is displaying some humility. At any rate
when the others (taking their cue from Olivia's diagnosis of
midsummer madness) torment him by pretending that he is
possessed by a devil, treating him like a child, and suggesting
that he rejects godliness, then the humour certainly begins to be
uncomfortable. Sir Toby wishes to have Malvolio bound as a
madman in a dark room, and to pursue the device until he tires
of it, while Maria, rather more spitefully, wishes to have Malvolio
expelled from the house, which will then be 'the quieter' (line
133).

The deception of Malvolio becomes positively cruel when
Feste plays his part, in the dungeon scene (IV.2), though Sir
Toby and Maria find it hugely enjoyable. Feste's disguised voice
(the visual disguise of gown and beard seems intended for the
audience, as Malvolio cannot see him) deceives Malvolio into
thinking that he is Sir Topas, but Malvolio stoutly refuses to
accept any of Feste's deceptions or blatant lies. It is not very
clear whether Feste is trying to drive Malvolio into genuine

madness, or merely trying to amuse the others, and himself. Sir Toby wishes to end the knavery here, though not out of compassion for Malvolio, but rather because he has offended Olivia so much that he cannot safely pursue the sport to a conclusion. Feste, however, knows no restraint, and his further tormenting of Malvolio in his own person — 'how fell you besides your five wits?' (IV.2.86) — seems more hurtful than ever. Although Feste keeps up his pretence that Malvolio is mad to the end of the play, Malvolio's appearance in the final scene arouses our sympathy rather than derision, as he asks *why* he has been made 'the most notorious geck and gull/ That e'er invention played on' (V.1.341–342). Olivia recognises the 'practice' in the forged handwriting, and is sufficiently moved to appoint Malvolio plaintiff and judge of his own case. It is left to the least guilty of the conspirators — Fabian — to claim that the device was contrived 'Upon some stubborn and uncourteous parts' (line 359) in Malvolio. Both Olivia and Orsino remain conspicuously sympathetic — 'He hath been been most notoriously abused' (line 376). Perhaps Fabian's curiously contradictory phrase 'sportful malice' (line 363) sums up our ambivalence towards the whole of this deception.

Not only the comic plot but the romantic plot is constructed on deception, some deliberate, some accidental. The first deliberate deception is when Viola instructs the sea-captain to present her as a eunuch to Orsino, and to:

> Conceal me what I am, and be my aid
> For such disguise as haply shall become
> The form of my intent.

> (I.2.54–56)

Her purpose is very unclear here, but the device makes possible some wonderful complications later. The reference to the eunuch is conveniently forgotten for the rest of the play. Certainly Cesario is not perceived as a eunuch by any other character — quite the contrary. Olivia of course is accidentally deceived into love for the 'youth's perfections' (I.5.285), for she cannot penetrate the irony of Viola's protestation 'I am not that I play' (I.5.177), though Viola does claim to be a gentleman. This causes her to contrive the deception of the ring and to disguise her new-found love from Malvolio by referring to the 'peevish messenger'

(I.5.290). Viola is concerned at the rapid repercussions of her deception:

> Disguise, I see thou art a wickedness
> Wherein the pregnant enemy does much.
> How easy is it for the proper false
> In women's waxen hearts to set their forms.

(II.2.27–30)

Shakespeare is allowing Viola to utter very conventional wisdom here, which is not borne out in the play, for the women are less easily deceived than the men.

In Act III scene 1, Olivia apologises for the 'shameful cunning' (line 113) of the ring deceit, and her shame leads her to bare her soul quite openly to Viola. They come teasingly close to revealing the deception:

> VIOLA: . . . you do think you are not what you are.
> OLIVIA If I think so, I think the same of you.
> VIOLA Then think you right; I am not what I am

(III.1.136–138)

But this encourages Olivia to believe that 'Cesario' is deliberately trying to conceal his real love for her and thus reveals her passion for him. At the end of the scene Viola cleverly tells the truth, but without revealing her secret, by stating that no woman has her heart and no woman would ever be mistress of it except 'I alone' (line 157). Similar subtle irony is employed in Act II scene 4, where the audience is fully aware that Viola is deceiving the Duke in claiming to love a woman of the Duke's complexion and years, and yet is declaring the truth of her love at the same time.

The deception produced by Viola's disguise is further cleverly complicated by the device, a favourite of Shakespeare's, of having identical twins dressed identically. Thus is made possible Antonio's fury at Viola's ingratitude in not returning the purse (lent to Sebastian simply to set up the scene), and his accusation of her being a model of deception:

> . . . the beauteous evil
> Are empty trunks o'er-flourished by the devil.

(III.4.361)

Viola's apparent dishonesty and cowardice then provoke the second challenge from Sir Andrew, culminating in the thrashing from Sebastian. Sebastian himself is aware that there is something in his extraordinary situation 'That is deceivable' (IV.3.21), but shows few scruples in enthusiastically welcoming his luck and hastily becoming betrothed to Olivia.

In the final scene the deceptions multiply furiously right up to the denouement, as Viola finds herself the target of a barrage of accusations. Antonio rails against her 'false cunning' (line 84); Olivia feels herself 'beguiled' (line 137) by 'Cesario's' appearing to be homosexual and declaring a sincere love for the Duke; (she quickly explains this away as deception produced by fear on 'Cesario's' part); Orsino is incensed to learn that 'Cesario' is betrothed to Olivia — 'O thou dissembling cub' (line 162), who practises the 'craft' of deception; and finally Sir Andrew comically reports that 'Cesario' is the 'very devil incardinate' (lines 178–179).

The audience of course is never really concerned for Viola's safety, for we have all the knowledge denied to those on stage. For them it is not until less than 200 lines from the end of the play that the situation is suddenly clarified with the arrival of Sebastian, and very quickly all the apparent deceptions are satisfactorily unravelled. Sebastian neatly explains to Olivia that nature, by providing identical twins, has actually *prevented* a deception:

> Nor are you therein, by my life, deceived:
> You are betrothed both to a maid and man.

> (lines 259–260)

I have shown, then, that the whole of *Twelfth Night* is a brilliant fabrication of deceptions, producing wonderful complications of plot and of characterisation. Unlike many devices which Shakespeare employs in other comedies, such as magic potions, fairies, transformations, deception is essentially an aspect of real life, and those who practise deceit here are ordinary people, not professional tricksters. The use of deception therefore helps to give *Twelfth Night* a reality and concreteness that is one of its most admired characteristics.

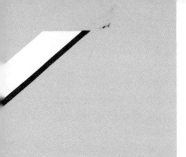

AFTERTHOUGHTS

1

Would 'The Deceptions' have been 'arguably a more appropriate title than "Twelfth Night", and certainly a better subtitle than "What You Will"' (page 40)?

2

Do you see Orsino finally 'as a fit husband for Viola' (page 42)?

3

What 'purpose' (page 47) do *you* see in Viola's original decision to disguise herself?

4

What relationship between deception and self-deception does this essay propose?

Paul Oliver

Paul Oliver is a member of the English Department and Director of Drama at Forest School.

ESSAY

The corruption of language in *Twelfth Night*

Whether you view *Twelfth Night* as a festive play with a melancholy undertone or a play in which the festive and the grimly realistic are awkwardly held in balance, there's no doubt that the characteristically bantering style of its language is what contributes more than anything else to our impression of the play as festive. This style is established very early — even before the play's 'allowed fool' (I.5.89), Feste, appears:

> MARIA   By my troth, Sir Toby, you must come in earlier o'nights. Your cousin, my lady, takes great exceptions to your ill hours.
>
> SIR TOBY   Why, let her except before excepted.
>
> MARIA   Ay, but you must confine yourself within the modest limits of order.
>
> SIR TOBY   Confine! I'll confine myself no finer than I am.
>
> (I.3.3–9)

This is punning on the most basic, crudest level: potentially ambiguous but contextually unambiguous words are deliber-

ately misunderstood, their other meanings substituted and ex-
ploited with a view to frustrating the intentions of the original
speaker. Maria, though, refuses to be sidetracked, being the
down-to-earth sort she is. All the more wonder, then, when she
quickly joins in the clowning on Feste's first appearance:

> MARIA   You are resolute, then?
> FESTE   Not so neither, but I am resolved on two points.
> MARIA   That if one break, the other will hold; or if both break,
>   your gaskins fall.

(I.5.20–23)

Feste's reply to this punning on the part of Maria, 'Apt, in good
faith, very apt' (I.5.24), seems to acknowledge that he feels that
he is being played at his own game or, rather, what would be his
game if this were almost any other play of Shakespeare's. It is a
special quality of *Twelfth Night* that riddling is anyone's game:
puns are dangerously contagious. Against this background, Feste
acts as a sort of facilitator or liberator of other people's wit. This
is certainly what is going on in his exchange with Viola in Act
III scene 1. Feste puns on the two meanings of 'live by' (live
near; make a living from) when Viola asks him if he is a
musician, which inspires her to pun on alternative meanings of
'lie by' (live near; go to bed with) and 'stand by' (stand near; be
supported by). Even Feste seems alarmed by this tendency of
puns to spawn puns: 'To see this age! A sentence is but a
cheveril glove to a good wit; how quickly the wrong side may be
turned outward!' (III.1.11–13). The use of a passive verb here
may serve to conceal Feste's professional annoyance at other
people playing tricks with words, but the image of a glove being
turned inside out is revealing because it clearly affirms that it is
possible to distinguish between 'right' and 'wrong' uses of language and, indeed, that there is such a thing as fixed meaning
in the first place. Yet the whole thrust of Feste's discourse is in
entirely the opposite direction: it tends constantly to subvert
meaning, to undermine the certainty other speakers feel that
what they are saying is basically unambiguous, as with Viola's
innocent question, 'Dost thou live by thy tabor?' (III.1.1–2). More
than anyone else, Feste by his use of language assigns to it just
that quality of autonomy which he seems here to be deploring.
   Of course, the remark about the glove is itself part of an

exchange of banter between the two characters, but this is a play where many true words are spoken in jest, and the same basic idea of the nature of language lies behind Feste's self-definition a few lines later. When Viola asks 'Art not thou the Lady Olivia's fool?' (III.1.30), he replies 'I am indeed not her fool, but her corrupter of words' (III.1.34–35). But, naturally, for there to be the possibility of corruption, there has to be stability in the first place.

Feste and Viola don't in fact share the same view of language. Viola's 'They that dally nicely with words may quickly make them wanton' (III.1.14–15) suggests that she sees playing with words as a deliberate and conscious human game, and an essentially self-indulgent one. Feste, however, views instability as inherent in language itself: 'words are very rascals' (III.1.19–20); 'words are grown so false' (III.1.23). He implicitly rejects the accusation of self-indulgence contained in Viola's remark. The truth surely lies exactly in the middle: Feste (repeatedly) and other characters (with varying degrees of frequency) exploit the instability of language for whatever happens to be their purpose at the time (to be amusing, to make money, to assert superiority, to evade the issue...); Viola's charge has to be levelled at her own linguistic practices as well as other people's.

So subversive are some of Feste's word-games that nonsense rather than ambiguity is the result: 'for Malvolio's nose is no whipstock, my lady has a white hand, and the Myrmidons are no bottle-ale houses' (II.3.25–27). Even if the separate parts of this extraordinary sentence all make sense (and it's certainly not been demonstrated satisfactorily that they do), the combination, though entertaining, is baffling. That this is an acceptable aspect of fooling is shown by Sir Andrew Aguecheek's response to this piece of non-meaning: 'Excellent! Why, this is the best fooling, when all is done' (II.3.28–29). If Feste's words quoted here seem an extreme example of the descent into meaningless-ness with which I am crediting him, there is nevertheless a circularity, and hence a lack of communicable substance, in numerous instances where our attention is distracted by some other feature of the utterance. Speaking to Sir Toby outside Malvolio's prison, Feste attributes the saying 'that that is, is' to an authority invented by himself, the old hermit of Prague, and comments: 'So I, being Master Parson, am Master Parson; for what is "that" but "that"? And "is" but "is"?' (IV.2.14–16). We accept the repetition here because, even without recourse to footnotes, we are bound to spot that Feste is making fun of a certain type of philosophical discourse. But it's quite meaningless and it's not surprising that Sir Toby's reply is the functional 'To him, Sir Topas' (IV.2.17). What possibility is there of engaging with Feste's words? Now watch something very similar happening in a less obvious example:

> ORSINO I know thee well. How dost thou, my good fellow?
>
> FESTE Truly, sir, the better for my foes, and the worse for my friends.
>
> ORSINO Just the contrary: the better for thy friends.
>
> FESTE No, sir: the worse.
>
> ORSINO How can that be?
>
> FESTE Marry, sir, they praise me — and make an ass of me Now my foes tell me plainly, I am an ass; so that by my foes, sir, I profit in the knowledge of myself, and by my friends I am abused. So that, conclusions to be as kisses, if your four negatives make your two affirmatives, why then, the worse for my friends and the better for my foes.
>
> ORSINO Why, this is excellent.

> (V.1.9–23)

Similar, because the amplification of the original statement actually adds nothing to it — and because the original statement is itself virtually pointless. But in this instance we're distracted by the dim sense that something is being proved and also by Orsino's 'this is excellent' (reminiscent of Sir Andrew's admiring remark earlier). It's noteworthy that in the process of 'proving' his statement, Feste uses linguistic terminology — frivolously, of course, but then the frivolity contributes to the overall meaninglessness of the speech. In other words, he draws attention at this point to what he's doing with language and is using *language rather than meaning* to amuse. Riddles of this sort bring us even closer than the puns do to language employed for its own sake. The puns, after all, are essentially a means of tilting the balance of power, stealing an initiative, in at least part of a given conversation.

Once we're alert to the nature of Feste's speech, it can throw light on how other characters speak, even when they're so concerned with the content of what they're saying as to be unaware that their speech is potentially bantering. Orsino is an excellent example of a man who is out of control emotionally and whose language shows a corresponding tendency to fly away with itself:

> CURIO Will you go hunt, my lord?
> ORSINO What, Curio?
> CURIO The hart.
> ORSINO Why, so I do, the noblest that I have.
> O, when mine eyes did see Olivia first,
> Methought she purged the air of pestilence.
> That instant was I turned into a hart,
> And my desires, like fell and cruel hounds,
> E'er since pursue me.
>
> (I.1.16–24)

Orsino's punning on hart/heart and his picking up of the conveniently offered raw material for an image of a man tormented by his desires is, if we're honest, exactly the same trick as Feste later indulges in. If it's too early in the play for the pun to alert us, the simile 'like fell and cruel hounds' should be enough to make us realise what is going on. Language is gaining a momentum of its own, and the only real difference between Orsino here and Feste and others elsewhere is that the speaker here is not out to entertain his hearers but to nourish his own sense of hurt. We wouldn't think of this as clowning or fooling, but isn't that mainly because of the absence of a third party other than the practical nonentity, Curio? We're back to Viola's 'They that dally nicely with words may quickly make them wanton' (III.1.14–15).

Orsino has often been characterised as being in love with love: perhaps it would be more helpful to think of him as in love with the language of love. That is certainly the impression given by his first few speeches. He does not, naturally, talk in this way the whole time (presumably no one could), but we are prepared by the non-reflective quality of his language for his inconsistency in, for example, saying first that men's 'fancies are more giddy and unfirm/ . . ./ Than women's are' (II.4.33–35) and a little later that 'There is no woman's sides/ Can bide the beating of so strong a passion/ As love doth give my heart' (ll.4.92–94).

Feelings, not perceptions, shape Orsino's utterances. The extravagance of his language should also do something to prepare us for his greatest inconsistency — the one he commits in giving up his claim to Olivia and staking one to Viola with the words 'Boy, thou hast said to me a thousand times/ Thou never shouldst love woman like to me' (V.1.264–265). However much the multiple marriages of the ending are determined by the play's comic structure, we are not prevented from commenting on the behaviour of individual characters — on the way Orsino switches allegiance here, for instance. (In the same way, the structurally conditioned ending of *Measure for Measure* does not require us to be blind to the Duke's highhandedness as he claims Isabella for himself.)

We learn a good deal about Orsino from the contrast between him and Viola, whose sufferings, though for the most part endured more privately, are more intense or at least have more tangible causes. Whereas Orsino's first words open up a whole world of potential for self-imposed pain, Viola's first words are practical — 'What country, friends, is this?' (I.2.1) — and then a highly rational attempt to surmount misfortune by affirming that it may not in fact have occurred:

> VIOLA And what should I do in Illyria?
> My brother, he is in Elysium.
> Perchance he is not drowned. What think you, sailors?
> CAPTAIN It is perchance that you yourself were saved.
> VIOLA O, my poor brother! and so perchance may he be.
>
> (I.2.3–7)

The punning on 'perchance' (perhaps; by a stroke of luck) has a very definite and positive effect: Viola introduces the possibility of Sebastian being alive tentatively; the Captain shifts the emphasis to the matter of being *saved*, at the same time, by his insistence on the literal meaning of the word, hinting at the operation of a beneficent fortune; Viola's second use of 'perchance' then appears to call on both meanings in asserting (almost) the *probability* of what she would like to be the case. From this point onwards she is active, but it is interesting to see the change taking place over the course of a single speech. Nothing could be more different from Orsino's dallying with the hart/heart pun — but it is a question of language as well as temperament. It's a linguistic strategy in the first place which enables Viola to become emboldened. Of course, our awareness of what is happening in scenes like this one is sharpened by the exchange between Feste and Viola in Act III scene 1: indeed, our memory of the punning on 'perchance' is almost certain to surface at that point.

If I seem to have laboured the centrality of the Feste/Viola dialogue, it is because it not merely articulates a theory of verbal clowning but comes close to a theory of language in general. Feste is the mouthpiece for a view of language which testifies to its slipperiness while acknowledging our total dependence on it:

> FESTE But indeed, words are very rascals, since bonds disgraced them.
> VIOLA Thy reason, man?
> FESTE Troth, sir, I can yield you none without words, and words are grown so false, I am loath to prove reason with them.
>
> (III.1.19–24)

The trap of language: words distort meaning and yet they're our only carriers of it. (Even gestures, postures and movement, the rest of drama's stock-in-trade, are used to reinforce language, to support or contradict what a speaker is saying and, in any case, all these are 'decoded' linguistically — as if they were verbal language.) It's a problem which has fascinated modern philosophers, challenging and exasperating them by turns. Nietzsche saw language as trapping and falsifying reality. What's interesting is that Feste had spotted this almost three centuries beforehand. We tend to recognise it as true but act as though it isn't. Professional corrupters of words, however, are paid to exploit the possibility of corruption.

I referred earlier to Feste's view that language is inherently unstable. Perhaps it would be more accurate to say that he sees language as tending towards ever greater instability: 'But indeed, words are very rascals, *since bonds disgraced them*' (III.1.19–20, my emphasis); 'words *are grown* so false' (III.1.23, my emphasis). It's a pity we don't know exactly what the first of these two statements actually refers to. Commentators have suggested that it hints at the practice employed by Jesuit priests at their trials of equivocating (saying one thing but meaning another) or, alternatively, that the reason why vows and pledges are now so important is that a gentleman's word is no longer his bond. But Feste's phraseology moves the attention away from any human agency behind the distortion and puts it firmly on language itself, a process continued in his next speech. All the same, we're given a clear picture of language as a social phenomenon, affected (like its users) by change and uncertainty.

We see Feste paid on four occasions in the play, twice for fooling and twice for singing. And since his singing is clearly an important part of his function as an entertainer, it's worth looking at the language of the three complete songs which he performs solo. (The chances are that all three are Shakespeare's work as opposed to popular songs of the day, but the impossibility of being sure about this does not affect considerations of their language and mood at all.) His first song begins 'O mistress mine! Where are you roaming?' (II.3.37) and is surprising on several counts. To begin with, it is entirely unambiguous. Of course, to expect the words of a song to be characteristic of the singer in some semi-autobiographical way would be to deny an important feature of song in general: its impersonality. The singer is a mouthpiece for the 'already written' (a phrase used by the critical theorist Roland Barthes to refer to all literary creation), and his hearers may do what they like with the song, as indeed may the singer himself. But it is true that Feste's two functions of singer and riddler pull in opposite directions — in the direction, we could say, of meaning on the one hand and nonsense on the other. Secondly, the song, though tender ('Trip no further, pretty sweeting') and neatly resonant ('Present mirth hath present laughter') is essentially trite: 'What's to come is still unsure'. No question here of the singer being paid for offering his hearers new perceptions. (Perhaps this is why Sir Andrew and Sir Toby praise the performance rather than the material.) Thirdly and most noticeably, the song's tone is grimly realistic and deeply pessimistic: 'Youth's a stuff will not endure'. This last characteristic is lost on Feste's audience, for whom the song appears to act as a tonic: the play's melancholy strain exists for the theatre audience and a small number of characters only.

Feste's second solo number, 'Come away, come away, death' (II.4.50–65), is a bleak piece which moves on from the possibility of uncooperativeness on the part of the woman implied by 'O mistress mine!' to an absolute certainty of it: the speaker of this second song, wasted by unfulfilled longing, wishes for and expects death. Dense with traditional emblems of death, it's a plea for annihilation and the obliviousness of those who outlive him every bit as complete as that contained in Henchard's will when he stipulates that 'no mourners walk behind me at my funeral and that no flowers be planted on my grave and that no man remember me' (*The Mayor of Casterbridge*, chapter 45). Only the song's impersonal nature and the safe, deathless context prevent the felt effect from being the same. (Many scenes in the play as well as its overall comic structure make it indisputably life-affirming.) But again the language of the song is highly conventional.

The final song, 'When that I was and a little tiny boy' (V.1.386–405), pushes the triteness several steps further. The cliché of its structure as it runs through the various stages of the speaker's life, and the repetition of the fourth line asserting the essential greyness of life, threaten to impair the impact badly. But how different is the song's effect in the theatre! The context (the ending of the play, the exit of the newly matched couples, the sense that Feste is shut out from the general happiness, being a visitor to both households but inmate of neither) contrives to make the play end on a note which is at least as much painful and disturbing as celebratory: the song, in other words, works powerfully *against* the ending appearing trite. Linguistically this is the hardest song to pin down. It's clear, as the speaker reviews his life, that he feels some sense of disappointment or, at least, of being pitted against larger, more enduring and basically hostile forces: 'For the rain it raineth every day'. The continuation, though, of the idea of each stanza into the succeeding one makes the word 'but' at the start of the second, third and fourth puzzling: the difficulty of following it through logically makes this the most suggestive and allusive of the songs, as though Feste wished to leave us with an impression of himself more consistent with what we see most of the time: a purveyor of riddles and things half-understood, half-hidden, a man who enables perceptions to be released but whose stance is often surprisingly defensive: the repeated references to the rain as well as the greater impersonality of the final stanza serve ultimately to deflect attention away from the singer.

The song is the closest we get to Feste in soliloquy, and no wonder: a Feste communing with himself is unthinkable precisely because one of his functions is to reflect the moods of others, and another is to supply people (Orsino, Sir Toby, Sir Andrew) with a mood which they self-indulgently crave but need someone else to provide. Viola comments to the audience on how he has to be shrewd and tactful: 'He must observe their mood on whom he jests' (III.1.60). But being all things to all men, is Feste ever himself? It's an irrelevant question: it's useless to expect 'personality' from a character who exists so much in terms of the functions he performs. But if I were forced (under torture) to stick a label on Feste, it would have to say that he acts as both a theoretical and practical centre for the play's linguistic strategies and, indeed, is the prototype (in drama) for all literary creations who use language self-consciously, subversively or banteringly. For some time yet he is bound to seem a curiously up-to-date character.

AFTERTHOUGHTS

1

'This is a play where many true words are spoken in jest' (page 53). Do you agree?

2

What do you understand by 'Feelings, not perceptions, shape Orsino's utterances' (page 56)? Do you agree?

3

Does the play as a whole support Feste's 'theory of language' (page 57)?

4

Compare Oliver's discussion of Feste's songs (pages 58–60) with Saunders's (pages 33–34).

Susie Campbell

Susie Campbell is Head of English at the North Westminster School. She is the author of several critical studies.

ESSAY

'The knave counterfeits well: a good knave': gender and disguise in *Twelfth Night*

'Disguise, I see thou art a wickedness', says Viola ruefully in Act II scene 2 of *Twelfth Night*. Despite this realisation, however, she does not question her own wisdom in continuing with her disguise as Cesario. She keeps it up in the face of Olivia's deception and increasing unhappiness, and her own painful role as Orsino's love-envoy. Why? She has seen its dangers, admits its possible 'wickedness', and there is no convincing external reason for it. Certainly, it is important to the story that she maintain the illusion that she is a boy. It is the central confusion around which Shakespeare weaves the web of misunderstandings and mistakes that make up the basic plot. It is also the most important of the several disguises and deceptions that run through the play. Others include Feste's impersonation of Sir Topas and Maria's forgery of Olivia's handwriting. But does Viola's disguise — and in particular the gender change it involves — have any further significance? Is Shakespeare making a point about gender itself?

Women disguising themselves as boys was a popular device in Renaissance drama and narrative. Shakespeare himself had already used it in several of his earlier comedies. In *As You Like It*, for example, Rosalind disguises herself as Ganymede, a shepherd boy, and inadvertently wins the love of Phebe, a shepherdess. Critics have argued over the significance of Shakespeare's use of gender-disguise as a dramatic device. In the Arden edition of *Twelfth Night* T W Craik insists that Viola's disguise as a boy is simply another instance of Shakespeare working within a well-established tradition. He sees the function of the disguise as 'artistic', helping to maintain a 'lightness of mood'. However, other critics have read much more significance into it. Ruth Nevo, for example, in *Comic Transformations in Shakespeare* (1980) reads the play as a comedy of sexual identity, with Olivia, Orsino and Viola all in a state of 'disequilibrium regarding masculine and feminine roles'; a disequilibrium corrected at the end of the play by Sebastian's appearance and the sorting out of confusions that ensues. In *Shakespeare Our Contemporary* (London, 1965), Jan Kott is less cautious. Illyria is 'a country of erotic madness', its theme 'erotic delirium or the metamorphoses of sex'. This is extreme and depends to some extent on his assumption that the audience would be highly conscious throughout the play of the fact that the female roles were played by boy-actors. This, for him, adds an extra level of ambiguity to Viola's gender-disguise and Olivia's attraction to him/her. Kott's discussion of *Twelfth Night* is stimulating reading but is, I suspect, too 'modern' in its response to the use of boy-actors in Shakespeare's theatre. The use of boys to play women's roles was a long-established convention and therefore less 'visible' to Elizabethan audiences than to twentieth-century critics.

The most challenging of the critical readings of Viola's gender-disguise is that by Catherine Belsey. In her essay 'Disrupting sexual difference: meaning and gender in the comedies', she points out that the sixteenth and seventeenth centuries were a period of crucial change in the whole position and 'meaning' of the family as a social unit. The definition of 'femininity' is strongly tied to the definition of the family, she argues, and was therefore undergoing important changes in this period. Belsey suggests this might account for the popularity of the themes of gender-disguise and reversal in Renaissance literature: 'The period of Shakespeare's plays is also', she reminds us, 'the period of an explosion of interest in Amazons, female warriors, roaring girls and women disguised as pages'.

By looking at *Twelfth Night* in this context, she produces a radical reading of what Shakespeare is up to. She sees this play as challenging or fragmenting the 'unity of the subject', that is, the idea that each person is a separate, whole self with a separate, whole gender identity. Viola as Cesario, she argues, is not necessarily either masculine or feminine. By thus throwing into confusion the whole idea of the fundamental difference between the genders, *Twelfth Night* quite radically challenges the sexual stereotypes of 'masculine' and 'feminine':

> that contest [for the meaning of the family] momentarily un-fixed the existing system of differences, and in the gap thus produced we are able to glimpse a possible meaning, an image of a mode of being, which is not asexual or bisexual, but which disrupts the system of differences on which sexual stereotyping depends.
>
> (*Alternative Shakespeares*, ed. J Drakakis, London 1985)

This range of critical opinion suggests that Viola's disguise is a complex and unsettled issue. But I find all the above views unsatisfactory, firstly because they do not pay sufficiently detailed attention to the text itself, and secondly because they tend to focus on questions about 'femininity'. If anything, it is 'masculinity' that is at issue in *Twelfth Night*. A close look at the scenes in which Viola's disguise is central leads to some interesting conclusions.

In Act I scene 2, Viola first assumes her disguise. Interestingly, this immediately follows her remarks to the sea-captain about the disparity that may exist between someone's outward appearance and their inner nature. Commenting on his outward seeming, she says warily:

> And though that nature with a beauteous wall
> Doth oft close in pollution, yet of thee
> I will believe thou hast a mind that suits
> With this thy fair and outward character.
>
> (I.2.49–52)

The possibility of being deceived by outward appearances is a theme that recurs throughout the play. Yet, despite her awareness, Viola chooses to accentuate the disparity between her inner and outer self. She bids the Captain: 'Conceal me what I am'. She has decided to enter the Duke's service and instructs the Captain, 'Thou shalt present me as an eunuch to him'. That the choice of word 'eunuch' is deliberate is emphasised by the Captain repeating it: 'Be you his eunuch, and your mute I'll be'. The Captain's suggestion that he take on the part of a mute adds further significant emphasis. In order to act out this role, the Captain would have to give up the power of speech. The way that the line is balanced brings the notion of a eunuch and that of a mute together as some kind of equivalent, underlining the sacrifice of power — this time, sexual power — implied by becoming a eunuch. This is intriguing. Viola seems to fear that her disguise may involve a 'castration' or loss of power. This is the opposite of what most critics assume. They see Viola's disguise as a gain, an extension of her personality and a *liberation* from the confines of her femininity. Their readings depend on our usual assumptions about the power-balance between men and women, whereby for a woman to become a man should be a gain not a loss. How can we make sense of this presentation of Viola's male-disguise as a 'castration'?

Is it that Viola fears that she will lose a determinate sexual identity by assuming the disguise? She is not really a man, nor is she actively a woman. As Belsey argues, she is occupying a position that is neither masculine nor feminine. But rather than this being the positive experience that Belsey's reading might imply, it seems to involve a loss of power. Without some kind of fixed gender identity, the play here implies, we are unable to participate fully in the arena of sexual encounter and competition. Interestingly, Viola does not carry out her intention of disguising as a eunuch but, on the contrary, plays Cesario as a virile young man. From very early on in the play, it seems, Shakespeare is raising questions and complications about gender and outward appearances. Already, T W Craik's argument that Viola's disguise is merely an 'artistic' device is not enough.

Act I scene 4 is important because in it Orsino chooses Viola as his representative to Olivia. Like Viola, he is aware of the distance between the outer, 'public' self and an inner, private

c

self, available only to confidantes. He says to Viola, 'I have unclasped/ To thee the book even of my secret soul (lines 13–14). Surrounding the theme of disguise, there is a wider theme of the putting on of social behaviour as the assumption of an identity, a public mask or disguise.

Orsino deliberately chooses Viola–Cesario as his ambassador because of 'his' youthful, and more particularly, feminine appearance. 'All is semblative a woman's part' (line 34), notes the Duke. Is this just dramatic irony so that the audience can enjoy Orsino's blindness to the truth, or is there a deeper irony here? Orsino believes that Cesario is the best choice for his emissary *because* of his girlish looks. He is convinced that male romantic love is best presented with a feminine aspect. Ironically, by choosing Viola to be his representative, Orsino places a question mark over his own masculinity and raises a wider question: if a man in love is best represented by a woman, what does it mean to be a man? This is a question picked up comically by Malvolio's attempt to act the lover. For Malvolio, to be a man and to be a romantic lover results in being taken, at best, for a buffoon, at worst, for a madman. His simpering and hand-kissing, his persistence in the face of Olivia's distaste parody Orsino's own love-sick behaviour and deepen the difficulty of finding a positive answer to the problem of being a man in love.

When, in Act I scene 5, Viola as Cesario first calls on Olivia, the latter seeks to find out what kind of man he is. 'What is he at the gate, cousin?' she asks, and again, 'What is he?' 'What kind o' man is he?' she asks Malvolio, 'What manner of man?' and again, 'Of what personage and year is he?' Nobody can give her a satisfactory answer. 'Why, of mankind,' Malvolio manages in reply to 'What kind o' man is he?' Olivia persists, asking Cesario himself, 'What are you? What would you do?' Her household's, and even Cesario's, inability to answer Olivia make tangible the play's own comic struggle to define a man. As I argued earlier, the question of what is a proper *masculinity* is a far more central question in this play than the nature of femininity. Any easy answers are thrown into disarray by the presence of Viola as Cesario who neither looks nor sounds like a man but is accepted by all as one.

This too is a theme that is picked up comically — this time, by Sir Toby and Sir Andrew. Running through their exchanges is an assertion of what proper manliness is. According to Sir Toby, it is machismo, exemplified in drinking, swearing and fighting. He urges Sir Andrew to fight Cesario, arguing, 'there is no love-broker in the world can more prevail in man's commendation with woman than report of valour' (III.2.34–36). Not for Sir Toby, Orsino's faith in girlishness as the key to male success in love. He advises, 'a terrible oath, with a swaggering accent sharply twanged off, gives manhood more approbation than ever proof itself would have earned him' (III.4.176–179). Sir Toby's opinions, of course, are self-serving and cynical. Sir Andrew who is to conform to this pattern of manliness is a coward and a fool, Sir Toby's puppet or 'manikin', while Sir Toby himself is a parody of the very 'macho' image he commends.

As the first meeting between Olivia and Viola as Cesario progresses, the former becomes increasingly interested in Orsino's emissary, proving further that it is no use looking to a romantic relationship between a man and a woman for an answer to the question 'What is a man?' The part of the male lover can be played as successfully by a woman as by a man. Viola realises with wonderment, 'I am the man' (II.2.25), as she discovers Olivia's feelings for Cesario.

The scene of Olivia and Cesario's first meeting is also important because it includes the first discussion of femininity — or, at least, femininity as constituted by female beauty. This arises when Cesario asks to see Olivia's veiled face. Olivia shows it as though it were a picture:

> . . . we will draw the curtain and show you the picture. [*Unveiling*] Look you, sir, such a one I was this present. Is't not well done?

> (I.5.223–225)

In answer to Cesario's praise of her beauty, Olivia inventories it as so many items:

> I will give out divers schedules of my beauty. It shall be inventoried, and every particle and utensil labelled to my will. As, item: two lips, indifferent red; item: two grey eyes, with lids to them; item: one neck, one chin, and so forth.

> (I.5.233–237)

Mock-humility or not, Olivia seems quite detached from her own feminine beauty — as it is detachable from her. She later gives Cesario her picture to wear (III.4). Her beauty seems to mean no more to her than a counter to be used in a game. She regards it as no more essentially her than Viola's disguise is Viola. Certainly, it cannot say anything about what femininity is — as is evident from the fact that Viola possesses female beauty and yet is taken for a man.

Interestingly, whilst several characters in the play are accused of 'unmanly' behaviour, no one is accused of being 'unfeminine'. Both Antonio and Sebastian worry lest they behave in an unmanly way. Sebastian, on the verge of tears, says to Antonio, 'my bosom is full of kindness, and I am yet so near the manners of my mother that, upon the least occasion more, mine eyes will tell tales of me' (II.1.35–37). Antonio himself says to Cesario:

> Do not tempt my misery,
> Lest that it make me so unsound a man
> As to upbraid you with those kindnesses
> That I have done for you.
>
> (III.4.340–343)

Fabian speaks disparagingly of Sir Andrew as a 'manikin' (III.2.51) and Sir Toby is so worried about the latter's ability to sound 'manly' even in writing that he decides to deliver the challenge to Cesario verbally so that he can 'set upon Aguecheek a notable report of valour' (III.4.187–188). On the other hand, the most Olivia is ever accused of, in her pursuit of Cesario, is jeopardising her *social position*. Viola chides her, 'you do think you are not what you are' (III.1.135). Viola herself escapes all reproof for her disguise. Never once is her lack of femininity deplored. Indeed, she wins Orsino's love precisely by acting in contradiction to what he sees as feminine behaviour. In the final scene he says to her:

> . . . for your service done him
> So much against the mettle of your sex,
> So far beneath your soft and tender breeding,
> And since you called me master for so long,
> Here is my hand
>
> (V.1.318–322)

In her important monologue in Act II scene 2, Viola reflects on the nature of gender. Realising that Olivia has fallen in love with her impersonation of a man, she says, 'Poor lady, she were better love a dream' (line 26). She then proceeds to speak disparagingly of the frailty of women with their impressionable 'waxen hearts'. The concept of femininity implied in this is that it is moulded around men, passively receiving its definition from the imprint of masculinity. With masculinity itself undefined, femininity too becomes uncertain.

However, whilst femininity, like masculinity, lacks any stable definition in this play, the comedy arises largely out of the confusion and anxiety surrounding the question of 'manliness'. This is inevitable given the view of femininity put forward by Viola as derived from masculinity.

With all the difficulty now surrounding gender, Viola reminds us in her monologue of the other problem posed by the play concerning sexual identity. Viola, who lacks a determinate gender, describes herself as a 'poor monster'. This returns us to the beginning of the play with its view of gender indeterminacy as a 'castration'. What was then a problem facing Viola alone has become, with the impossibility of defining masculinity and femininity, a universal problem.

The final scene that I want to discuss in any detail is Act II scene 4, in which Orsino and Viola as Cesario discuss gender. At the beginning of the scene, the Duke, who is already moodily unsure of how to be a masculine lover, tries to make a virtue of his own uncertainty. It is the way of all true lovers to be 'Unstaid and skittish' (line 18), he claims. (This is later knocked down by the Clown, who ridicules the Duke's 'opal' mind). Orsino then questions Cesario about the boy's own beloved. Viola replies by describing the one she loves in terms of Orsino himself:

DUKE   What kind of woman is't?
VIOLA   Of your complexion.
DUKE   She is not worth thee, then. What years, i'faith?
VIOLA   About your years, my lord.

(II.4.26–28)

There is dramatic irony here, of course. The audience enjoys Viola's tightrope around the truth and the Duke's credulity. There is also, as we by now expect, a deeper irony. By describing 'his' beloved — supposedly a woman — in terms of Orsino, a man, Cesario perpetuates the uncertainty around the definition of gender difference that runs through the play. This seems to disturb the Duke, who responds by reasserting the difference between the sexes. He evokes established conventions. Women are 'roses', beautiful but frail, strong only in their love for men. Their husbands or lovers should be older because men are more swayed by their passions and therefore less inclined to be faithful. Viola agrees. Women's whole purpose is to bloom and die (there is innuendo here, 'die' bearing a double meaning of death and sexual orgasm) for love.

Ironically, Feste's song contradicts this definition of gender difference completely. It portrays man as a passive, frail creature who 'dies' of love:

> Come away, come away, death,
>   And in sad cypress let me be laid.
> Fie away, fie away, breath!
>   I am slain by a fair cruel maid.

(II.4.50–54)

Orsino's next attempt to define a man in love assimilates the Clown's song and completely reverses his previous definition:

> There is no woman's sides
> Can bide the beating of so strong a passion
> As love doth give my heart; no woman's heart
> So big to hold so much, they lack retention.

(II.4.92–95)

He ends, 'Make no compare/ Between that love a woman can bear me/ And that I owe Olivia'; highly ironic, seeing as he is saying this to a woman that the audience knows loves him at least as much, if not more, than he loves Olivia. Viola counters his assertion with the story or parable of her own faithfulness and endurance in love and points out that mere macho swaggering proves nothing.

The scene ends where it began, with all the attempts to define gender difference in disarray, as Viola answers the Duke:

> I am all the daughters of my father's house,
> And all the brothers too

(II.4.119–120)

A riddle with a profound multiplicity of truth. By this stage in the play it has indeed become impossible to segregate gender in any permanently meaningful way.

The end of the play resolves the issue on a superficial level. The fortuitous reappearance of Sebastian clears up the various confusions and ensures that the right partners end up together. But on a deeper level, nothing is resolved. Sebastian contributes to the equivocation around gender by assuring Olivia that she is marrying a 'maid and a man', leaving the only significant difference between himself and Viola the ability to wield a sword. As we know from the rest of the play, not all men are natural fighters so this ability cannot be a reliable measure of gender. Meanwhile, the Duke persists in calling Viola 'Boy' and 'Cesario' even after he has discovered that she is a woman. He seems quite happy to conflate the affection that he feels for his page with the romantic passion he sees as the proper feeling for a man to have for a woman.

The play ends with the Clown's song, in its own way a cynical answer to the question 'What is it to be a man?' Growing up as a man, the song suggests, only brings worry, self-doubt and dissolution. Not even the knowledge that 'swaggering' doesn't 'thrive' can help. A man's life ends in impotence and dotage.

Returning to Belsey's analysis of the play, I must disagree with her emphasis. The play is not so much dissolving or disintegrating gender identity, as she argues, as showing the irresolvable difficulties inherent in trying to define masculinity and femininity in the first place. Again Belsey's reading is too modern in perspective. It assumes that gender was already defined and fixed by Shakespeare's day. This play suggests otherwise, that gender was only conceived of in very broad terms and that new attempts to define and separate the sexes were comical in their folly. This might lead us to a pessimistic conclusion. The play seems to be offering the negative message that the determinate sexual identity it sees as essential for success in love can never be achieved. However, Viola's experience is not so negative. The impotence that she fears will follow upon her assumption of a disguise turns into a new kind of power as she wins first Olivia's love, then Orsino's, through her successful performance as Cesario. This returns us to the other theme of the play — the need to act a part or put on a public mask to participate in society. When Feste disguises himself as Sir Topas he argues that he is only doing as others do: 'I would I were the first that ever dissembled in such a gown' (IV.2.5–6). If ultimately all social behaviour is an act, then gender becomes part of the performance. The issue is then one of how successfully the performance is delivered and who is directing it.

Neither Sir Andrew nor Malvolio are good actors, nor do they direct themselves. They are manipulated into playing parts they have not chosen and they fail, Malvolio as the romantic lover, Sir Andrew as the courageous fighter. Viola and the Clown, on the other hand, choose (or in Feste's case, knowingly assent to) their own roles and play them well. Viola knows full well that disguise has its perils but she is in control and acts out her chosen role brilliantly. She is rewarded for her dramatic success, somewhat surprisingly, with the love of Orsino. Malvolio, on the other hand, is punished for his thespian ineptitude. Acting prowess seems to be a more significant determinant of success than moral worth for characters in this play. As Sir Toby says of the Clown, we might say of Viola: 'The knave counterfeits well: a good knave.'

AFTERTHOUGHTS

1

Should modern productions of *Twelfth Night* cast boy-actors to play the female roles?

2

Do you agree with Campbell's argument that 'masculinity' rather than 'femininity' is the central issue in *Twelfth Night* (page 64)?

3

Would *you* agree that 'male romantic love is best presented with a feminine aspect' (page 66)?

4

Do you agree that 'Acting prowess seems to be a more significant determinant of success than moral worth for characters in this play' (page 72)?

Michael Gearin-Tosh

*Michael Gearin-Tosh is Fellow and
Tutor in English Literature at St
Catherine's College, Oxford. He is also
Associate Director of the Oxford School
of Drama.*

ESSAY

The world of
Twelfth Night

In the last scene of *Twelfth Night* Shakespeare took the unusual
step of recalling an earlier moment in the play. Olivia expresses
sympathy for Malvolio:

> Alas, poor fool, how have they baffled thee!
>
> (V.1.367)

Feste, however, is bitter and taunting. He reveals who Sir Topas
was and continues:

> But do you remember: 'Madam, why laugh you at such a barren
> rascal, an you smile not, he's gagged'? And thus the whirligig of
> time brings in his revenges.
>
> (V.1.371–374)

This alludes to Act I scene 5 when Olivia asks:

> What think you of this fool, Malvolio? Doth he not mend?
>
> (I.5.68–69)

Malvolio disagrees:

> I marvel your ladyship takes delight in such a barren rascal . . .
> unless you laugh and minister occasion to him, he is gagged.
>
> (I.5.78–82)

The incidents balance each other. In both Olivia expresses sympathy, and for a 'fool'; in both she provokes a hostile reaction. We shall come close to the heart of *Twelfth Night* if we consider each of these moments in its context.

Act I scene 5 opens with Feste asking Maria to help him get his job back. She refuses. She wants to know where Feste has been and he will not tell her. Indeed, the audience never finds out. Nor do we know why he left, although we can speculate. Feste was 'a fool that the Lady Olivia's father took much delight in' (II.4.11–12). Both father and son died in the months before the play starts. In her grief, Olivia came to rely on Malvolio's sombre orderliness:

> He is sad and civil,
> And suits well for a servant with my fortunes.
>
> (III.4.5–6)

Did she forget to tell Feste that she also valued him? Was he too unconfident of her affection to know that she wanted him to stay, that she might need him? Did Malvolio make some unfeeling remark?

Whatever the cause, Feste left, and Olivia bridles when he reappears: 'Take the fool away'. She even sounds like Malvolio for a moment:

> Go to, y'are a dry fool. I'll no more of you. Besides, you grow dishonest.
>
> (I.5.36–37)

Feste tries to placate her with the quibbles of traditional clowning. They fall flat. The only course left is the unexpected. Nobody, least of all a servant, said to a countess of her brother:

> I think his soul is in hell, madonna.
>
> (I.5.63)

It must have outraged Malvolio. If the gambit failed, would there have been a position for Feste in Illyria? But Olivia is big enough to like Feste making a fool of her, and she laughs more than for a long time — perhaps it is the first real laughter since her father's death.

Malvolio's response is ungenerous to Feste, but we dislike it for more than that. Olivia has not only laughed at Feste. She has laughed at herself. And she has laughed with Feste in the fun and exhilaration of his triumph. Comedy is performing one of its high functions. It checks her sorrow. It enriches her sense of her own life. It celebrates acute good sense in that its cause was Feste's point about her lack of true belief in heaven, with the implied consequence that if she believes in God, she should have hope for her own life. Olivia's laughter signals the release of her affection for Feste and it re-establishes a precious link with the memory of her father. We feel that she is no longer one of those women whom Larkin described:

> Their beauty has thickened.
> Something is pushing them to the side
> Of their own lives.

> ('Afternoons', lines 22–24)

When Malvolio later rebukes Toby in the drinking scene, he is stopping a brawl. But with Feste and Olivia in Act I scene 5, he is opposing generosity, joyousness, expansion and precious memory, the spirit of comedy itself.

Comedies often include an anti-comic figure and the way in which that figure is handled can determine the stature of the play. Malvolio is not sinister. Unlike Don John in *Much Ado About Nothing*, for example, he never chills us with a sense of viciousness in reserve. Indeed, the most harm he can do — and he pays dearly for it — is what he threatens to Maria:

> Mistress Mary, if you prized my lady's favour at anything more than contempt, you would not give means for this uncivil rule. She shall know of it, by this hand!

> (II.3.117–120)

No doubt Maria was aware of what Fabian tells Toby about Malvolio:

> You know he brought me out o'favour with my lady about a bear-baiting here.

> (II.5.7–8)

Malvolio's power is his access to Olivia. But it is no more than that. In this sense he is less isolated than the anti-comic figures in Shakespeare's other comedies, and this influences our feeling about him. We experience a subtle combination of laughter at his idiocy, yet an awareness that Olivia, whom we love, values him.

We would respond differently to Malvolio if his antagonists were more attractive. Toby is a much lesser figure than Falstaff, Shakespeare's other drinking knight in the plays of these years; and if poor Olivia by some freak of fate was obliged to choose between her 'in house' suitors, is Andrew more desirable than Malvolio? The yellow-stocking scene obliquely invites us to consider Olivia in the arms of her bossy steward:

> OLIVIA Wilt thou go to bed, Malvolio?
> MALVOLIO To bed! 'Ay, sweetheart, and I'll come to thee!'
>
> (III.4.28–30)

This is very funny, but in a different way from our laughter with Olivia over Feste in Act I scene 5. There is a misunderstanding, of course, but our real laughter comes from the thrill of imagining a wildly improbable liaison. Once irregular laughter is unlocked, it is a potent force. In a subversive way, Malvolio the outrageous swiver gains stature, and we feel an anarchic geniality towards him. The letter scene has prepared for this. Many of us daydream, and daydreams are the common home of freakish, scarcely permitted thoughts. The intimacy of overhearing a person's daydreams also makes for warmth.

We do not laugh less at Malvolio for this geniality, but our laughter is more complex, our mood more alert. The presence of Toby, Andrew and Fabian also increases our sympathy for Malvolio, although without alienating us from them. We are with them because we feel Malvolio deserves a jape and we like fun. On the other hand, they are three to one, and Malvolio manages to score against his teasers, even if unknowingly:

> MALVOLIO Besides, you waste the treasure of your time with a
>   foolish knight . . .
> ANDREW That's me, I warrant you.
> MALVOLIO One Sir Andrew
>
> (II.5.76–79)

Another factor is Malvolio's headlong eagerness:

> I will be strange, stout, in yellow stockings and cross-gartered,
> even with the swiftness of putting on.
>
> (II.5.163–165)

This preening is little less than orgasmic. It is absurd. It can only come to grief. But vanity is common, and lust is natural even if linked with ambition. We might giggle at a timid prig, but are we against one who gallops to disaster?

Twelfth Night is fuelled by most powerful dynamics. Feste helps to awaken Olivia into a vitality which sweeps her away: she falls in love a few minutes later, and she pursues Cesario with impetuousness and courage. But Malvolio, although hostile to Feste and to comedy, is also aroused into a pursuit of love. In addition to this double action, the play has not one anti-comic force, but two. And the second is to be the most unexpected of all, the very source of comedy in Act I scene 5.

In the last scene of *Twelfth Night*, when Malvolio utters outrage at his treatment, we are invited by Fabian to make the type of measured judgement which is often thought to represent the cultivated good sense on which social life depends:

> Good madam, hear me speak;
> And let no quarrel, nor no brawl to come,
> Taint the condition of this present hour,
> Which I have wondered at. In hope it shall not,
> Most freely I confess, myself and Toby
> Set this device against Malvolio here,
> Upon some stubborn and uncourteous parts
> We had conceived against him. Maria writ
> The letter at Sir Toby's great importance,
> In recompense whereof, he hath married her.
> How with a sportful malice it was followed
> May rather pluck on laughter than revenge,
> If that the injuries be justly weighed
> That have on both sides passed.

(V.1.353–366)

Olivia, who consoled Malvolio before Fabian's speech, says only:

> Alas, poor fool! How have they baffled thee!

(V.1.367)

She is struck by the weight of the conspiracy against him. One of her own family has plotted against a servant. He was joined by the lady-in-waiting, her most intimate attendant, and by Fabian whose quick intelligence is manifest in his speech. Then she learns that there was still another persecutor.

It is not common for Shakespeare to reveal so much that is central to his characters in the last forty lines of a play (and they include twenty lines of song). The last lines of *Twelfth Night* deploy what might be called highly refined shock tactics. We learn that Malvolio had a power beyond his access to Olivia and that his crabbed joylessness could enter Feste's soul.

Malvolio's jibes in Act I scene 5 make theatrical sense only if Feste is paralysed for a moment:

> Look you now, he's out of his guard already; unless you laugh
> and minister occasion to him, he is gagged.

> (I.5.80–82)

'Going dry' is the comedian's trauma, and Malvolio has induced it. Feste describes his professional skill to Viola in Act 3 scene 1:

> You have said, sir. To see this age! A sentence is but a cheveril
> glove to a good wit; how quickly the wrong side may be turned
> outward!

> (III.1.11–13)

This facility was blocked by Malvolio — and that must have been unnerving. But we do not predict, I think, that Feste would resent it for so long: he was soon himself again, and the upset seems insignificant when set against his triumph with Olivia and his easy happiness with Orsino.

Feste's speech at the end of the play is very unkind. Malvolio is never going to be Count Malvolio and Olivia is married to Sebastian. Nor does it help Feste in our sympathies that he recalls Sir Topas. Fabian invites 'injuries' to be 'justly weighed'. Malvolio's prime offence to Toby was that he carried out Olivia's instructions. Maria said at the time:

> If my lady have not called up her steward Malvolio and bid him
> turn you out of doors, never trust me.

> (II.3.70–72)

Malvolio was pompous to Toby, but Olivia's instructions were likely to have been sharp. Nothing justifies the way in which Toby and Feste played games with Malvolio's sanity:

> They have here propertied me; keep me in darkness, send

ministers to me — asses! — and do all they can to face me out of
my wits.

(IV.2.91–93)

Fortunately he was too robust to be seriously disturbed. But
their treatment of him was sinister in a way that he is not. Feste
also continued as Sir Topas after Toby told him to stop (IV.2.65–
70, 95–101). No doubt Feste had suffered mental pain in Act 1
scene 5. But he is an artist, his talent is to create by turning a
'cheveril glove' outward and it is especially disagreeable when
people who live for the imagination, or by the imagination, act
negatively and meanly. We feel they should be above it. Malvolio
hurt Feste in part through coarseness. This is different from the
infliction of pain by a sensitive man.

Events move quickly in the final seconds of *Twelfth Night*
and Shakespeare allows no room for comment. But it is notable
that Olivia does not console Feste for his pain as she had done
Malvolio. Her response is a simple but eloquent cry:

He hath been most notoriously abused.

(V.1.376)

We accept Olivia as the voice of real discernment in the earlier
quarrel between Feste and Malvolio and we should do so here.
She does not attempt to strike a balance between the injuries of
Feste and Malvolio, as Fabian had done with those of Malvolio
and Toby. Making a fair judgement diverts us from whether we
should be judging at all, and throws a cloak of respectability
over an activity which is generally too detached to be loving.
Olivia sees that whatever the merits of Feste's case, his manner
undermines them. She acted as a peacemaker, he renews ill
feeling. And what are his motives? Feste humiliates Malvolio by
reminding him of his social ambitions in front of Olivia, Sebastian
and Orsino, where it could not be more embarrassing. There is
an element of personal flaunting. Feste is not content with
having played Sir Topas, he wants Malvolio to know who Sir
Topas was. All this has come from a clown whom she has
cherished and whose professional skills include a supposed
mastery of timing:

This fellow is wise enough to play the fool;
And to do that well craves a kind of wit.

He must observe their mood on whom he jests,
The quality of persons, and the time,
And, like the haggard, check at every feather
That comes before his eye. This is a practice
As full of labour as a wise man's art.

(III.1.58–64)

Shakespeare shows the affection in Olivia's cry by having her, no doubt unawares, use Malvolio's own word: 'He hath been most *notoriously* abused'. Malvolio used it twice in his speech of complaint to her (V.1.326–342), and he used it once before in the Sir Topas scene (IV.2.87). It is not used at any other point in the play. If we are sharp enough to notice, we may smile at Olivia sounding like Malvolio again for a moment.

One reason for the pace of the ending is to keep the mood light. Feste's song is brilliantly poised between the choric and the personal: we do not apply it wholly to the play — we can scarcely imagine Olivia saying 'But when I came, alas,' to marry — and we hope that Feste's inner life is not as desolate as that of the song. But he does sing the song alone. This is a departure from Shakespeare's earlier practice in the comedies: the song which ends *Love's Labour's Lost* is sung with everyone on stage. We like Feste, but we also recognise that those who seek revenge, as Bacon put it, 'do but trifle with themselves' as well as hurting others. There is a rightness in his isolation.

AFTERTHOUGHTS

1

What do you understand by 'anarchic geniality' (page 77). Do you agree with Gearin-Tosh's analysis here of audience response to Malvolio?

2

Do you agree that Olivia's pursuit of Cesario shows 'courage' (page 78)?

3

Is bad behaviour more blameworthy in the 'sensitive' (page 80)?

4

Do you agree with Gearin-Tosh's final judgement of Feste (page 81)?

Bill Alexander

*Bill Alexander is Associate Director of
the Royal Shakespeare Company. In
1987 he directed a production of* Twelfth
Night *at the Royal Shakespeare Theatre,
Stratford. His cast included Antony
Sher as Malvolio.*

ESSAY

'Why, we shall make him mad indeed': directing the 'dark room' scene (Act IV scene 2)

There's a great deal in *Twelfth Night* about madness. People often talk of the play as though it were a revels play — perhaps because of the association of its title with the Christmas festival. But, for all of its comedy and charm, I see it as very much darker than that. Like so many of Shakespeare's plays, it's about what happens to individuals when their idea of themselves prevents them from taking in the reality of the world around them. They act irrationally, lose their sense of proportion, become — in a way — unbalanced. And what happens to Malvolio is an obvious example of this. He takes himself too seriously, makes enemies by his insensitive handling of other people, and then is too insensitive to realise that a trick is being played on him. His vanity and self-importance are too great for him to react sensibly to the forged letter. And to Olivia, unaware of how he has been duped, his behaviour seems as crazy as that of a real madman: 'Why, this is a very midsummer madness' (III.4.56).

Perhaps that exclamation of Olivia's is what gives Sir Toby his idea for what follows, the imprisonment of Malvolio as though in a madhouse cell:

> Come, we'll have him in a dark room and bound. My niece is already in the belief that he's mad. We may carry it thus for our pleasure and his penance till our very pastime, tired out of breath, prompt us to have mercy on him; at which time, we will bring the device to the bar, and crown thee for a finder of madmen.

> (III.4.134–140)

Deciding quite how to set about staging this 'dark room' scene is a problem for actors, directors and designers alike. An audience will have divided sympathies when Sir Toby's plan is put into effect. Malvolio is humourless and unlikeable; yet his enemies' treatment of him seems monstrously unfair and out of all proportion to what he has actually done. For the director, as well as for the characters, it's a question of getting the balance right.

The idea of being taken to a dark place and physically confined was quite typical of the way a genuinely mad person might be treated by the Elizabethans, as it happens: their attitude to madness was much less sympathetic than nowadays — much more rough and ready, less squeamish. But the idea of staging a scene that focuses on someone locked up in a dark room has its special problems for a director. He or she has to decide how much or how little an audience is going to be able to see of the character.

The stage directions for the 'dark room' scene (IV.2) all imply that Malvolio is out of sight — he is described as speaking from 'within'. In an Elizabethan theatre he might have been speaking from behind a curtained recess, or from a trapdoor beneath the stage, and one way of playing the scene in a modern theatre is to put Malvolio under the stage, with just his hand appearing through some grating. This means that the actor playing Malvolio is expressing the whole dilemma of the character with his right hand and index finger. It's quite an effective way of doing it. In fact, it's the idea we first started out with, in rehearsals. But more and more productions are tending to try to find some way of putting Malvolio on stage. After all, the actor playing Malvolio only has five scenes altogether — it seems a bit of a shame for him to be physically absent from one of the most important ones. And my Malvolio had a strong preference for being up on the stage rather than under it.

Deciding to have Malvolio on stage for the scene creates another set of problems, though: because the text makes it very clear that he is not able to see Feste at all. If you do what some productions do and simply box him into some sort of on-stage prison — a kind of telephone kiosk without windows — and have him shouting from inside it, then you might just as well have left him under the stage. The audience will not be seeing any more of him. But if you bring him on stage suffering from some other kind of confinement — in a straitjacket, maybe, or even in a wheelchair — then he is also going to have to have his hat jammed down over his eyes or be blindfolded, so as not to see Feste.

Once we had decided that our Malvolio was definitely going to be on stage, we began first of all with the idea of his being blindfolded. Then, as we started rehearsing it in that way, we came up with the idea of his being chained to a post, just as bears used to be in bear-baiting. It fitted in with the suggestion we wanted to give of his being the victim of a cruel sport, of being tortured like an animal. And it also fitted in with the dialogue between Fabian and Sir Toby at the beginning of Act II scene 5. You find out then that one of the reasons why Fabian has a grudge against Malvolio is because he told Olivia that Fabian had been bear-baiting: 'You know he brought me out o'favour with my lady about a bear-baiting here' (II.5.7–8). And it's interesting that Sir Toby's immediate response to that is to suggest that Malvolio himself should be baited like a bear: 'To anger him, we'll have the bear again, and we will fool him black and blue' (II.5.9–10). That seemed to me an important visual image.

After that, once we had decided on the bear-post, one of the two actors playing Malvolio and Feste — I don't remember which — suddenly said, why didn't we actually set the scene in the dark room itself? We could let the audience see Feste descending a ladder, to make it quite clear that he was going down to join Malvolio in his prison cell. And that would mean that *both* of the two characters would be in the dark: *neither* of them would be able to see the other. There would no longer by any need to blindfold Malvolio — the room would be in pitch darkness.

That made a lot of sense. It also provided a way of explaining something that's always puzzled me, which is, why — if Malvolio cannot see him, and they are not even in the same room together — does Feste bother putting on a disguise to pretend to be Sir Topas? Why wouldn't it be enough just to alter his voice? If you have them stumbling around in the dark together, then of course it's more logical — Malvolio would be bound to reach out his hands in the direction of a voice and perhaps feel the false beard.

So we decided that we were going to set the scene actually *in* the dark room. That meant, of course, that we had to re-think what to do with Sir Toby and Maria, who are normally on stage for the first half of the scene. Originally, we had planned to have Sir Toby dancing around behind Feste, taking great delight in what was going on, with Maria egging him on. But now, instead of that, we decided to place the two of them up at the back of the stage, looking down from a tiny lighted window. We would have them embracing each other, kissing each other — clearly enjoying listening to Malvolio's distress and even seeming to get a perverse kind of kick out of it.

Staging the scene like that — with Sir Toby and Maria up at the window — gave us another way of reminding an audience that the action on the main stage was taking place below ground level. But it also gave us the chance to suggest something rather unsavoury about Sir Toby. One thing I'm sure of is that he's not the lovable ne'er-do-well that he likes to think himself. In fact, *no one* in *Twelfth Night* is quite what they seem or wish to seem! As I see it, he is an irresponsible wastrel who exploits everyone around him — Olivia, Sir Andrew and even (given their relative social positions) Maria. People often claim that his line in this scene: 'I would we were well rid of this knavery' (IV.2.66–67) shows that he's starting to feel sorry for Malvolio and guilty about what's going on. I have never seen it like that. He's a hugely insensitive man: why would Malvolio's suffering upset him particularly? Isn't it much more likely that he's simply getting worried about his own skin at this point? He's already in dreadful trouble with Olivia over the drunken revels. The trickery is all bound to come out sooner or later. He knows he had better not take it *too* far.

With the staging of the scene getting clearer all the time in our minds, we then started rehearsing in earnest. It involved a good deal of practice with blindfolds or in blacked-out rooms, as the actors playing Feste and Malvolio each learned how to play a sighted person who can no longer see anything; and it involved a great deal of discussions, for instance, about the sorts of fears one would have — of sharp objects, of falling down holes — and of the odd sensations that one would experience in touching something unexpectedly. And we learned a lot about the way the human voice changes in that sort of situation. It becomes higher, far more restrained in a strange way. But by far the most important thing to come out of those early sessions was an entirely new idea about how the scene itself might best be presented on the stage.

Up until then, we had been planning to play the scene with the stage in near-total darkness. We had been planning to deal with it naturalistically. Then suddenly someone remembered the *Black Comedy* idea. *Black Comedy* is a play by Peter Shaffer that takes place in darkness. But instead of being in darkness, the stage is in fact brightly lit — so that what the audience sees are people *behaving* as though it were completely dark. I suppose it's rather like those TV wild-life documentaries that film foxes and badgers by night with an infra-red camera so that you can watch what they are doing, even though normally you couldn't see them in the dark. Anyway, this technique seemed a perfect solution. Instead of dimming the whole stage, we would flood a certain area of it with dazzlingly bright light to delineate the dark room. Both Feste and Malvolio would have their eyes open. But it would be clear to the audience from the very first moment — by the way that they moved around the stage — that neither of them was able to see a thing. Every moment they made would be choreographed carefully.

The use of light in this way would heighten the farce of the scene. But it would also heighten its cruelty. Not a single wince or grimace would go unnoticed. Like so much of the play, there is a blend in this scene between humour and horror. Malvolio is not really mad in this scene. Nor — despite Fabian's hopes — does he *go* mad at this point. He hangs on desperately to his reason, and I think most audiences respect him for that. But there is still a certain 'mad' quality about the scene — in its snatches of song, its disguises, the sudden debate about Pythagoras and wildfowl. And the use of bright light to represent darkness would be one way of underlining that bizarreness.

It would also give an important continuity to the way I had already decided to use lighting in the production as a whole. As I said at the beginning, I see the play as being partly about what happens when people lose their sense of balance. I wanted to stress in my production some of the links between love and madness. And I wanted to show people behaving in ways that are extreme, or deluded, or uncharacteristic — slightly 'touched' perhaps. It was the thought of reasonably ordinary people behaving in ways that could be thought of as slightly 'touched' that gave me the idea of setting the play in a hot climate. Even though the action takes place nominally in Illyria, the characters could hardly be more English. And I thought of that Noel Coward song, 'Mad Dogs and Englishmen Go Out in the Mid-day Sun'. I wanted a sense of the intense Mediterranean heat that can go to people's heads. So the stage set was rather like a Greek island — white-washed houses, bright blue skies. A lot of people said it reminded them of pictures of Mikonos. And the lighting was deliberately strong when people's behaviour was at its most illogical.

We set the letter scene (II.2) at siesta time, for instance — the idea being that, instead of being sensible and lying in the shade or in the cool of his room, Malvolio is pacing around under the hot sun, with his mind going in a really bizarre direction as he fantasises about marrying Olivia. The people watching him are safely at a window, in the cool. He's alone in the heat. And the bright white walls of the buildings around him give the audience a visual suggestion that Malvolio is in a lunatic asylum all of his own, surrounded by white walls. Strong light becomes equated with madness. So by setting the 'dark room' scene in a cube of white light, we could not only recall that earlier scene but intensify its effect.

I mentioned earlier that we did not see Malvolio as at all mad when we worked on this scene. The situation might be mad. The world he lived in might be mad. But Malvolio himself was wretchedly and earnestly sane. That was part of the power of the scene. His state of mind in the final scene, though — when he's led back out into the daylight barefoot, dishevelled and shielding his eyes from the sun — seemed to us quite a different matter. He leaves the stage finally with the departing line, 'I'll be revenged on the whole pack of you!' (V.1.375). When and if that revenge came, would it be the action of a sane man or a madman?

AFTERTHOUGHTS

1

What advantages can you see in placing Malvolio off-stage for the 'dark room' scene (page 84)?

2

Do you see any links between the comments about bears in this essay (page 85) and Saunders's comments on Orsino's name (page 30)?

3

What reasons would you give for Feste's putting on a physical disguise to play Sir Topas (page 86)?

4

What advantages does this essay highlight of exploring a dramatic text through *performance*?

Peter Reynolds

*Peter Reynolds is Lecturer in Drama at
the Roehampton Institute, and author
of several critical studies.*

ESSAY

Illusion in Illyria: 'Nothing that is so, is so' (IV.4.9)

A myth most commonly associated with adolescence, but nonetheless a widely prevalent one, is that young people who claim
to be 'in love' are more often than not under an illusion. They
are in love with the *idea* of being in love rather than with
another person. A recognisable aspect of behaviour connected
with this state is a marked tendency towards self-dramatisation.
The 'lover' wears his or her condition as a clearly visible badge
for all to see. They tend to assume that their condition is of
overriding interest to everyone, not just to themselves. But, like
drunks, lovers are only really tolerable to other lovers. Sometimes this form of self-delusion, involves acting out the role of
spurned lover. All this dramatic activity is harmless enough
because most people grow out of it, and usually it affects no one
other than themselves. Such behaviour is associated with adolescence (perhaps unfairly) because that is a time when people
are thought to be between childhood and maturity and therefore
not yet fully in control of powerful feelings of adult sexuality,
nor fully in touch with the evolving sense of their adult selves. It

is a time to play out roles such as that of the lover in order to test out and explore the new freedoms and opportunities presented by adult life. Such self-dramatising illusions become problematic when the players can no longer distinguish between illusion and reality.

Shakespeare's *Twelfth Night* contains many characters who experience difficulties in distinguishing between illusion and reality: Orsino is one of them. The play begins with a scene very similar to the archetypical one I have outlined. It may be a critical cliché, but it is nonetheless true, that Count Orsino, whom the audience sees commanding music and speaking aloud of his unrequited love, is in love with love. However, he is no adolescent. Yet he apparently spends his time carefully manufacturing a self-indulgent narcissism, using music as a kind of sensual narcotic in order to induce feelings of what he labels 'love' for Olivia. Paradoxically this love causes him pain rather than pleasure, and his first words speak not of life, but of sickness and death:

> If music be the food of love, play on,
> Give me excess of it, that, surfeiting,
> The appetite may sicken, and so die.
> That strain again! It had a dying fall.

(I.1.1–4)

Thus, the most powerful man in Illyria, is shown as essentially passive, emasculated by his fixation on the object of his desire. His almost morbid fixation with his own plight echoes the popular Elizabethan stereotype of the lover, 'such as I am, all true lovers are:/ Unstaid and skittish in all motions else,/ Save in the constant image of the creature/ That is beloved' (II.4.17–20). It is also reminiscent of that other fashionable Elizabethan pose — that of the melancholy man. Orsino appears determined to play both parts to the full.

The traditional image of the melancholy man was familiar to Elizabethan theatre audiences through such characters as Jaques in *As You Like It*. He, you may remember, has no significant friendships with the other inhabitants of Arden, and, when Rosalind, Orlando and the other members of Duke Senior's court have left, remains in the forest, a determinedly solitary figure. Orsino too is cut off by his adopted condition from the

(margin annotation: music as sensual narcotic)

society of others ('I myself am best/ When least in company' I.iv.37–38). But of course Orsino's is an *adopted* condition. He possesses free will and has decided, although claiming he wishes to be 'cured' of his condition, deliberately to adopt this position in relation to the rest of the world. Of course by doing so he draws attention to himself as being 'special' and different from his peers, a classic sign of the kind of adolescent behaviour that is often the despair of parents!

In the opening scene of the play Orsino displays an unwillingness to respond to the prompting of his anxious courtiers to find a diversion in the traditional male pursuit of hunting. Hunting would mean joining with other men in a collective activity and Orsino has no wish to dissipate the effectiveness of his own self-dramatisation by sharing his stage with others. Traditionally the melancholy man prominently demonstrated his inner state by adopting the most conspicuous signs of outward display: a generally languorous air and a suit of black clothes. It may well have been the case in the first performances of *Twelfth Night* that, although there is no direct reference to it in the spoken text, the actor playing Orsino wore melancholy black. If this was so it makes an obvious but important link to the subsequent presentation of the object of his desire: Olivia.

Like Orsino, she too has cut herself off from society, and like him she also indulges in a degree of self-dramatisation. The audience have been told that, since the death of her brother, she has become like a nun: 'The element itself, till seven years' heat,/ Shall not behold her face at ample view,/ But like a cloistress she will veilèd walk' (I.1.27–29). To live as a nun was also to live a celibate life, and this is of course what causes Orsino most pain and what he finds impossible to understand. When the audience first see her, in Act I scene 5, they note that she has not as has been reported by the Captain 'abjured the sight/ And company of men' (I.2.40–41), but that she is highly selective about those men allowed in her company. She admits only those who pose no physical threat or temptation: Sir Toby Belch, Sir Andrew Aguecheek, Malvolio and Feste. In performance the colour of her veil, and perhaps even the colour of her dress, may have been black to signify her state of mourning for her dead brother and thus make an important visual link between her state and that of Orsino. Significantly, as Act I scene

5 rapidly makes clear, her position seems as contrived as that of the melancholy Duke. Within minutes of her first entrance her façade has been challenged by the Clown, who seeks leave to 'prove [her] a fool' (lines 52–53). He challenges the validity of Olivia's adopted role with a familiar but effective argument:

> FESTE Good madonna, why mourn'st thou?
> OLIVIA Good fool, for my brother's death.
> FESTE I think his soul is in hell, madonna.
> OLIVIA I know his soul is in heaven, fool.
> FESTE The more fool, madonna, to mourn for your brother's soul, being in heaven.
>
> (I.5.61–66)

Olivia's immediate response is to appear to recognise its validity: 'What think you of this fool, Malvolio? Doth he not mend?' (lines 68–69). But the real evidence that she is not altogether as committed to her role as she seems comes a few minutes later, when first Maria and then Malvolio bring her news of the arrival at her gate of a 'young fellow' (line 134) and she asks pointed questions as to the kind of man he is. On learning that he is both young and attractive the woman who has supposedly 'abjured the sight/ And company of men' (I.2.40–41) admits one.

Before Viola–Cesario enters, Olivia attempts to create an illusion in order to confuse Orsino's embassy: she throws the veil over her face in order to disguise herself. However, in the course of the encounter with 'him', Olivia rapidly shatters the illusion. She begins by discarding the outward sign of mourning; lifts her veil and displays her face to Viola–Cesario. She then confounds convention by demanding to be left alone with 'him', and, when they are alone, talks openly and flirtatiously with this new 'man'. By the end of the scene her old role has been dropped entirely in favour of a new one: Olivia is now in love not with the memory of her dead brother, but with Viola–Cesario: 'Even so quickly may one catch the plague' (line 284). The speed with which Olivia changes roles is characteristic of lovers in Shakespearean comedy, but Olivia's love, although perhaps deeply felt, is based not on truth but on a fiction: she is under the illusion that Cesario ('...I am not that I play', (line 77)) is a man.

There is of course a further twist in the complex illusions surrounding Olivia. When Viola's brother Sebastian makes his appearance in Act IV scene 1, she mistakes him for Viola–Cesario, and subsequently marries him. Thus she is deceived on three levels: first that she is wedded to the idea of her dead brother, second that she has fallen in love with a man, and thirdly that she has married Viola–Cesario.

Twelfth Night is a play that contains not only self-deception, but literal deception, especially in the extent of the cross-dressing of characters. Of course, Shakespeare's players were all male, and in the original casting of *Twelfth Night* presumably the players would have attempted to cast Viola–Cesario and Sebastian with two actors who not only resembled each other, but, in the case of the actor playing Viola, could also convincingly represent a woman. Olivia, in falling in love with Cesario and then later mistakenly thinking Sebastian to be 'him', seems to indicate that she finds a man who is so like a woman (his sister) to be immediately acceptable to her, whereas a more obviously 'manly' man, like Orsino, she has rejected. Perhaps it is male sexuality that she is afraid of; she certainly surrounds herself with men who are not in the least sexually attractive — Toby Belch, Sir Andrew Aguecheek, Malvolio. And when Malvolio does declare his desire it is treated, not least by Olivia, as a joke. Despite his overt expressions of unfulfilled desire, Orsino too only falls in love when sexuality is not an issue. For Viola's literal deception in representing herself as Cesario gives him time to be with her without the pressure of overt sexuality that would presumably be present if he knew of Cesario's gender. This deception presents him with an opportunity to get to know Viola, whereas he has had no opportunity to encounter Olivia. But, there is more than a mere suspicion in this play that, here and elsewhere, the shifting feelings of both Orsino and Olivia reveal two deeply insecure individuals, more at home with their own than the opposite sex, and who at times appear superficial and ultimately self-centred.

A third character who bears many of the hallmarks of Orsino and Olivia and suffers under many illusions, not least about himself, is Malvolio. He too has adopted black as a badge signifying his isolation and difference from others. Malvolio is a puritan (Maria: 'The devil a puritan that he is . . .', II.3.140), and the puritan's costume was largely black. Like Orsino and Olivia, Malvolio too keeps most people at arm's length. In Shakespeare's

England, and especially in London, the puritan's were a group who deliberately kept themselves apart from ordinary society, believing as they did in the certainty of their own salvation and the equal certainty of the damnation of the rest. They were powerful figures in the City of London and opposed to the playhouses. Because of the strength of their opposition the players were forced to build their theatres on the south bank of the Thames outside the jurisdiction of the City. It was generally thought that puritans were set against anything but hard work, and play-going certainly did not constitute work; indeed, as performances took place during the day it probably necessitated absence from work! Sir Toby's famous cutting remark to Malvolio, 'Dost thou think because thou art virtuous, there shall be no more cakes and ale?' (II.3.111–112) probably sums up a good deal of popular anti-puritan sentiment. But it is not only the wearing of black and the fact that his puritanism separates him from the everyday cut and thrust of society that links Malvolio with Orsino and Olivia: like them he lacks self-knowledge and enjoys playing a role. Malvolio's generally ill-disguised contempt for Sir Toby, Sir Andrew, and the rest of his mistress's household is based on feelings of superiority which have no basis in reality. He is under the illusion that he is naturally their moral superior.

He appears at his most ridiculous when, under the illusion that Olivia is in love with him, he plays the role of the lover — a part dictated by the script (letter) written for him not by Olivia, but by her maid, Maria. Malvolio lays himself open to such crude deception because, like Orsino and Olivia, he is self-deceived. Malvolio lacks self-knowledge and is 'sick', as Olivia says, of 'self-love' (I.5.85). He falls eagerly into the trap set by Maria to the delight of those gathered to watch him fall.

But it is not only Malvolio, Orsino and Olivia who are deceived or self-deceived in this play. Almost everyone in *Twelfth Night* is at some point under an illusion: Orsino that he is in love with Olivia; Olivia that she is married to the memory of her late brother; Viola that her brother is dead; Sebastian that Viola has perished; Malvolio that Olivia is in love with him; Sir Andrew that Olivia is in love with him; Antonio that Viola–Cesario is Sebastian; Sir Toby, Sir Andrew, Maria and Feste that Sebastian is Viola–Cesario, and so on. These illusions succeed not because they are skilfully and convincingly maintained, but because the people who apprehend them are all too easily taken in by fictions. Not only are people deceived by outward appearances, but also, and much more significantly, they are often self-deceived.

Twelfth Night as a whole seems to be a play about a decadent society where people's feelings are not to be trusted. Although it is supposedly a comedy, and certainly in the late twentieth century it is one of the most frequently performed of Shakespeare's plays, suggesting that it is well liked by actors and audiences, it is a play, I suggest, that presents an audience with a bleak picture of the human condition. The men and women portrayed within it are repeatedly revealed as shallow, foolish, and capable of extreme cruelty. Even the names of some of the characters — Belch, Aguecheek, Feste — seem to conjure the smell of decay. Indeed, the behaviour of Sir Toby, too often played as a genial Falstaffian figure of fun, is in reality very far from possessing that knight's qualities of generosity and common humanity. Sir Toby Belch is only too keen to exploit the trusting friendship of the simple Sir Andrew, and quick to resort to violence when encountering Sebastian. The world he inhabits seems closer to the empty and ultimately meaningless landscape of Samuel Beckett's plays than it does to the sunlit uplands of Shakespeare's other comedies. But unlike Beckett, where characters can redeem the apparent hopelessness of their situation through their capacity to laugh at themselves, the humour in *Twelfth Night* seems always to arise at the expense of another human being. We are invited to laugh at the gullibility and human frailty of Sir Andrew, to laugh at the drunken loutishness of the bullying Sir Toby, and to find it amusing that the so-called Clown subjects the imprisoned Malvolio to a form of mental torture in trying to convince him that he is mad. In *Twelfth Night* we almost never laugh *with* the injured party, but are encouraged instead to laugh *at* them.

Although superficially *Twelfth Night* resembles the other romantic comedies of Shakespeare, in that, in common with them, it contains pairs of lovers who suffer temporarily from cases of mistaken identity, and any confusion that results is resolved in the closing scenes — men and women are united in marriage and fools get their come-uppance — the general atmos-

D

phere of self-delusion and self-indulgence cannot entirely be erased by the concluding marriages. In the light of their behaviour as presented on the stage, the prospects for the forthcoming marriages of Orsino and Viola and Sebastian and Olivia do not look rose-tinted. Shakespeare seems disinclined to show that either Orsino or Olivia have learnt anything from their experiences, or from the fact that both have been grossly self-deceived. Unlike the lovers in *As You Like It*, who enter the Forest of Arden as adolescents and *use* the time to play out love-games in which they rehearse and test the behaviour required in adult married life, and consequently by the end of the play are recognised as mature, Orsino and Olivia seem locked into adolescent illusions.

The mood of the end of the play is therefore hardly celebratory. There are no dances, no collective celebration. Just as the action of the first scene began with one man listening to music, it ends with the audience themselves in the passive role of the consumers of Feste's lyrics. After everyone else has left the stage the Clown/Fool sings exactly the kind of melancholic song so beloved of Orsino. Far from travelling in the right direction towards enlightenment and personal happiness, the characters have gone nowhere . . . they and we have come full circle to the point where the action began. The ears of the audiences about to leave the theatre are filled not with a lyric in praise of love and marriage, but with one that echoes a bleak picture of the future, of going drunk to bed, walking together not into the sunset but into the rain because, in Illyria at least, 'the rain it raineth every day'.

AFTERTHOUGHTS

1

Do you agree that 'lovers are only really tolerable to other lovers' (page 91)?

2

What parallels does Reynolds draw in this essay between Orsino and Olivia (pages 93–95)?

3

Explain the relevance to Reynolds's argument of the reference to Samuel Beckett's plays (page 97).

4

Compare Reynolds's comments on the ending of *Twelfth Night* (pages 97–98) with Holderness's essay (pages 100–107).

Graham Holderness

*Graham Holderness is Head of the
Drama Department at the Roehampton
Institute, and has published numerous
works of criticism.*

ESSAY

Happy endgames

People often express a preference for 'happy' rather than 'un-happy' endings. Such a preference is often coupled with a wry acknowledgement that happy endings to novels or dramatic comedies are not 'realistic': that they belong to a realm of fantasy in which the suffering, the misery and the intractable difficulties of 'real life' are temporarily banished or smoothed over. Happy endings in the theatre compensate us, perhaps, for the obvious and familiar fact that the 'stories' of real people's lives do not always turn out so cheerfully. In a more sober and resigned frame of mind we may admit that tragedy provides a more accurate assessment of the chances of life, a more realistic acceptance of its ultimate outcomes. One way of telling the 'story' of Shakespeare's life as a dramatist is to propose that he favoured the genre of comedy when possessed by a spirit of optimism, and veered towards tragedy as his outlook on life clouded, saddened and 'matured'.

Since all life ends with death, tragedy may be regarded as a true and accurate reflection of the nature of 'ending'. All life doesn't 'end' with marriage and reconciliation and forgiveness, as dramatic comedies do. But then life doesn't 'end' in any way at all, never comes to a stop, except with death. So there is something paradoxical about the two elements of the term 'happy ending'. Surely happiness is something we associate with stability, continuity, the assurance of unalloyed pleasure; if it comes to an 'ending', then we are being delivered over to the arbitrary diversity of real life, with its characteristic mixture of pleasures and pains.

Where dramatic comedy is associated (as it is in *Twelfth Night*) with the experience of revelry, celebration, carnival — where attending the play is like being at a party — the prospect of its *ending* can only be regarded with regret, sadness, with the restlessness of unfulfilled desire. Watching a comedy in a theatre, we can temporarily inhabit, for the duration of the play, a world in which people can experience adventure without coming to harm, take risks with a guarantee of ultimate luck, turn themselves and their world upside-down with an assurance that things will always right themselves. For a permitted space we imaginatively occupy a world full of pleasure, liberty, fun, harmless excitement. When it comes to an end, however happily, we are turned out of the theatre into a real world where such purity of pleasure has no independent existence: a world where it rains, where the bus we are waiting for doesn't come, where loss and separation and denial are as much a part of life as love and fooling and celebration. Shakespearean comedies often compare themselves to the kind of pleasant dream from which awakening is a matter of regret. In *The Tempest* Caliban speaks of such dreams, visions of a haunting beauty that make waking an experience of loss: '. . . when I woke, I cried to dream again'. Here a beginning (waking to reality) is also an ending (of the dream). A 'happy ending' may thus entail the ending of happiness.

Twelfth Night 'ends' with restoration, reconciliation and unity. A brother, a sister, a friend, who have lost one another, are all found. Misunderstanding is cleared up, identity restored: Sebastian is recognised as himself (not 'Cesario'), 'Cesario' can turn her assumed masculine disguise inside out to reveal her true feminine self. The comic sub-plot is disclosed, and Malvolio released from his bondage. The members of the cast are largely organised into heterosexual couples (Viola/Orsino, Olivia/Sebastian, Sir Toby/Maria), so the convention of marriage is employed to re-align the characters into an orderly configuration, free from disguise, transsexual relationship and misapprehension. Orsino's final speech links these various associations firmly together:

> When . . . golden time convents,
> A solemn combination shall be made
> Of our dear souls. Meantime, sweet sister,
> We will not part from hence. Cesario, come;
> For so you shall be, while you are a man.
> But when in other habits you are seen —
> Orsino's mistress, and his fancy's queen!

(V.1.379–385)

The comedy closes in the perpetual sunshine of a 'golden time', with social integration and unity ('combination'). Gender differences are clarified — 'Cesario' will now reassume her own woman's clothes — and in the light of those re-established distinctions, relationships are 'straightened out' — the woman Orsino was pining for, Olivia, is safely placed at a distance by a fraternal affection ('sweet sister'); and Viola can relinquish all her adopted masculine characteristics to become assimilated into Orsino's conventional romanticism ('his fancy's queen'). There will be no more loss, no more misunderstanding, no more separation: 'we will not', says Orsino on behalf of the unified collective, 'part from hence'.

Orsino's affirmation of happiness shared in perpetuity is clearly an attempt to establish a 'happy ending'. But in one sense, at least, he is wrong: since the narrative structure embodied in the dramatic text immediately requires all the actors to 'part from hence'. They may not part one from another, but on the irresistible command *'Exeunt'* they are parted from their audience: their happiness becomes our ending. We go our separate ways ('you this way, we that way'), the characters to a projected eternity of assured fulfilment, we back to the real world where such a conception can only ever be a haunting dream.

But this is not quite the 'end'. Between the departure of the characters and our own departure from the theatre there is a transitional moment, occupied by Feste's song. Dramatically a song can be performed as an integrated element of the theatrical narrative, as in an opera or musical; or it can be performed directly to the audience, as an additional piece of entertainment that is not quite part of the narrative proper. In the first instance, we perceive the song as an expression of the character, and a contribution to the dramatic atmosphere: it remains firmly 'inside' the play. The other characters may applaud the singer, but the audience in the theatre doesn't think to interrupt the flow of narrative by clapping. Sometimes in stage productions, on the other hand, songs are separated from the dramatic situation in which they appear, so that momentarily the actor turns aside from the dramatic action and sings to entertain us, the audience; the theatrical narrative is temporarily suspended while we listen to the actor as a professional performer, a singer rather than a dramatic character. Songs which appear earlier in the play, such as 'O mistress mine' (II.3.37–50) and 'Come away, come away, death' (II.4.50–65), could obviously be performed in the first of these conventions: they are thematically related to the play's central concerns; the songs are commissioned by the other characters themselves; the characters comment, applaud and reward the singer.

Feste's final song seems to require a different convention, since it appears in a different context: the other characters have all left the stage, so there is no one for Feste to sing to except the theatre audience. The song could be performed as a kind of soliloquy, a moment of quiet self-communing. But is the song really an expression of Feste's 'character'? And what function could it have in the dramatic narrative? Furthermore, the internal evidence of the song itself indicates that it could not be performed entirely in this way. It may begin apparently as Feste's autobiography, but it ends with the singer resolving from a character into an actor, a professional performer who declares that the stage illusion has come to an end: 'our play is done' (V.1.404). There is a projected continuity, as the actor offers to the audience the services of himself and his company: 'we'll strive to please you every day' (V.1.405). But the promise that the illusion may be subsequently recreated does not entirely compensate for its immediate loss.

Furthermore, if we look more closely at the song itself, we can observe that it is a melancholy little reflection on the intrinsic unhappiness of endings. Looking back to childhood, Feste recalls a time when 'play' was innocent and unproblematical: when pranks and folly needed no justification, being acceptable as innocuous fun appropriate to the status of a child — 'A foolish thing was but a toy' (V.1.388). For the adult however, all that has changed: the irresponsibility of folly in a grown man is regarded as unacceptable, threatening and subversive; the adult who wants to continue playing games is regarded as a criminal, and excluded by authority from civilised society, displaced to the margins of social life — ''Gainst knaves and thieves men shut their gates' (V.1.392). Adulthood marks an end to the liberated irresponsibility of play. So too does marriage: when the man comes to 'wive' (V.1.394) he encounters another limit, since the immaturity of blustering folly ('swaggering', line 396) evidently gets him nowhere in the battle of the sexes. This cynical view of marriage as the imposition of unwanted responsibility casts an oblique perspective on the centrality of marriage in the play as a symbol of concord and resolution.

It is difficult to understand what the fourth stanza means, but we can conjecture that it is an allusion to the kind of revelry, habitually practised by Sir Toby, which represents a hopeless attempt to sustain the irresponsible innocence of childhood. As the drunken reveller is put to bed, he enacts a grotesque parody of childlike dependence. In the last stanza any sense of 'beginning' — the origin of the world, birth and childhood, the freshness of the new — is too far away to contemplate:

> A great while ago the world began,
>> With hey-ho, the wind and the rain;
>> But that's all one . . .

$$(V.1.402-4)$$

'That's all one', a phrase that recurs throughout the play, signifies from one perspective that, since nothing is really important enough to worry about, pleasure and folly are the only activities worth undertaking — 'who cares', 'so what', 'what the hell'. From another perspective, only slightly removed from the first one, the phrase can be read as hopeless, despairing resignation: if nothing matters, pleasure and folly can only ever be doomed attempts to escape from an intolerable consciousness of emptiness and futility. The latter suggestion is certainly present in the phrase that follows: 'our play is done' (line 404). Literally this means simply that the play *Twelfth Night* is over. But as the song began with a wistful recollection of the purity of childhood 'play', the phrase seeks a more general application: 'play'-time is over; it is time to grow up; the anxiety and resignation of adulthood must be reassumed. Outside the charmed circle of the stage, outside the licensed revelry of the theatre, 'the rain it raineth every day'. The players will do everything they can to soften or dispel that disenchanted awareness, but they too are adults, and so their 'playing' can never be free from anxiety: 'we'll *strive* to please you' (V.1.405, author's italics).

'I am sure', Sir Toby affirms at the beginning of the play, 'care's an enemy to life' (I.3.2). Yet the song with which the play closes seems to confirm that 'care' is the very condition of 'life'; and that to be 'careless' is not to be 'carefree', but to be engaged in a continual hopeless effort to keep the inevitability of anxiety at a distance. Is life then its own enemy, self-divided against its own deepest and most passionate needs? Are play and pleasure locked into an irreconcilable antagonism with the anxiety that threatens them? If this is so, then it throws a very interesting light on the whole play: since (aside from Feste's song) the one character who professes belief in the necessity of anxiety is the one character who is excluded from the otherwise universal harmony of the play's conclusion: Malvolio. Malvolio, bitterly disillusioned and (in Olivia's words) 'notoriously abused' (V.1.376), has excluded himself from the compact of cheerfulness and gaiety secured by the rest of the cast. Possessed by a vindictive rage, he unites both those who have fooled him and those to whom his own folly has been exposed, in a comprehensive passion of indignation: 'I'll be revenged on the whole pack of you!' (V.1.375). He places himself outside the newly integrated community of the play, and casts a shadow over its delicately achieved balance of concord and reconciliation: which, we recognise, has been attained only at the cost of ejecting an unassimilable fragment. Even in his absence, his painful alienation and his oath of vengeance brood ominously over the play's closure; and there at the margins of the drama, his bitter and disappointed presence seems to meet the chastened resignation of the Clown, stranded alone with his own melancholy music, evidently no more a part of the collective celebrations than is Malvolio himself.

I said Malvolio 'professes' the necessity of anxiety because, of course, the authenticity of his puritan credentials are obviously questioned. It is Maria who identifies Malvolio as 'a kind of puritan' (II.3.134); and it is in the guise of an authoritarian kill-joy that he interrupts the revelry of Act II scene 3. But Maria herself immediately denies that Malvolio's puritanism consists of any seriously held moral or religious convictions: 'The devil a puritan that he is, or anything, constantly, but a time-pleaser' (II.3.140–141). Malvolio is not so much a historical portrait of a seventeenth-century puritan, as an example of the stage convention which portrayed puritans as hypocrites, cloaking their own lust and mendacity under a façade of moral respectability. When in fantasy he imagines himself Olivia's husband or consort, there is no shortage of pleasure imagined for his own consumption (II.5.46–48).

But if care truly is both life's implacable enemy and life's inescapable antagonist, then Malvolio can be regarded as a central figure in the play. His fate is to be duped with false hopes and tempted with illusory aspirations; to experience disillusion and disenchantment; and finally to be diagnosed as mad, bound, confined, and eventually released to endure the open mockery of his captors and the suppressed amusement of his superiors. In the light of Feste's song, and of the ambivalent nature of the play's 'happy ending', Malvolio can obviously stand as a representative figure in that inhospitable world where even innocent folly is punished and excluded. He is of course a victim of poetic justice, since he was a self-appointed instrument of that universal anxiety, dedicated to the identification of folly in others, and the systematic denial of folly in himself. He is in the end, after all, only forced to exhibit the foolishness he shares with others. Yet although foolishness, irresponsibility and the hopeless pursuit of perpetual pleasure are all common characteristics — they are certainly central to the character of Orsino, and Olivia is not free from them — Malvolio is the only character to be punished for his participation in a common destiny. He is the scapegoat, the victim who bears away with him the sins of the community. Perhaps the ritual is only a game, and Malvolio may be entreated back to join the party.

Or perhaps not. As the Clown stands alone, outside the official revelling of a united court, looking towards a disenchanted world where the rain rains every day, Malvolio's threat of revenge may begin to assume a shadowy substance and a menacing shape. Those who invest their existence in the expectation of perpetual pleasure, guaranteed happiness, the uninterrupted continuance of the game, will always be exposed to the resentment and resistance of those acquainted with anxiety, who are no strangers to grief. Although I have said that Malvolio is no historical portrait of a puritan, it remains a tempting possibility (pursued by some stage productions) that his banishment and threatened revenge may correspond to the marginalisation and eventual victory of the puritans who were later to fight against the King in the Civil War. Perhaps for Duke Orsino too the whirligig of time might have brought in his revenges. But that would be another play (*Malvolio's Revenge?*), a hypothetical tragedy which lies quite beyond, though it is paradoxically shadowed by, the 'happy ending' of *Twelfth Night.*[1]

---

[1] This essay is considerably indebted to Nick Potter's discussion of *Twelfth Night* in Graham Holderness, Nick Potter and John Turner, *Shakespeare: Out of Court* (London, 1990).

AFTERTHOUGHTS

1

What significance can you see in the title of this essay?

2

On what grounds does Holderness argue that a 'happy ending' may 'entail the ending of happiness' (page 101)?

3

Compare Holderness's comment on Malvolio's puritanism (page 106) with Reynolds's (pages 95–96).

4

What do you imagine might happen in *Malvolio's Revenge* (page 107)?

A PRACTICAL GUIDE TO ESSAY WRITING

INTRODUCTION

First, a word of warning. Good essays are the product of a creative engagement with literature. So never try to restrict your studies to what you think will be 'useful in the exam'. Ironically, you will restrict your grade potential if you do.

This doesn't mean, of course, that you should ignore the basic skills of essay writing. When you read critics, make a conscious effort to notice *how* they communicate their ideas. The guidelines that follow offer advice of a more explicit kind. But they are no substitute for practical experience. It is never easy to express ideas with clarity and precision. But the more often you tackle the problems involved and experiment to find your own voice, the more fluent you will become. So practise writing essays as often as possible.

HOW TO PLAN
AN ESSAY

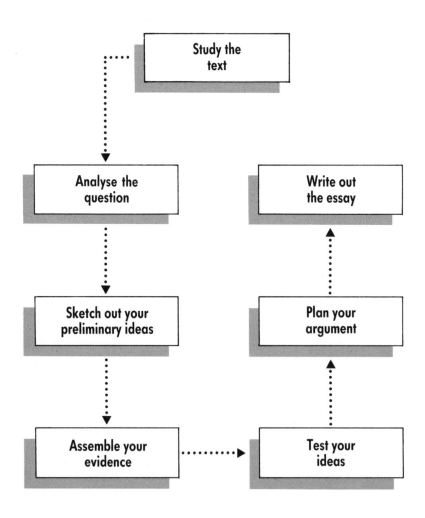

Study the
text

Analyse the
question

Write out
the essay

Sketch out your
preliminary ideas

Plan your
argument

Assemble your
evidence

Test your
ideas

Study the text

The first step in writing a good essay is to get to know the set
text well. Never write about a text until you are fully familiar
with it. Even a discussion of the opening chapter of a novel, for
example, should be informed by an understanding of the book as
a whole. Literary texts, however, are by their very nature
complex and on a first reading you are bound to miss many
significant features. Re-read the book with care, if possible more
than once. Look up any unfamiliar words in a good dictionary
and if the text you are studying was written more than a few
decades ago, consult the *Oxford English Dictionary* to find out
whether the meanings of any terms have shifted in the inter-
vening period.

Good books are difficult to put down when you first read
them. But a more leisurely second or third reading gives you the
opportunity to make notes on those features you find significant.
An index of characters and events is often useful, particularly
when studying novels with a complex plot or time scheme. The
main aim, however, should be to record your *responses* to the
text. By all means note, for example, striking images. But be
sure to add *why* you think them striking. Similarly, record any
thoughts you may have on interesting comparisons with other
texts, puzzling points of characterisation, even what you take
to be aesthetic blemishes. The important thing is to annotate
fully and adventurously. The most seemingly idiosyncratic
comment may later lead to a crucial area of discussion which
you would otherwise have overlooked. It helps to have a working
copy of the text in which to mark up key passages and jot down
marginal comments (although obviously these practices are
taboo when working with library, borrowed or valuable copies!).
But keep a fuller set of notes as well and organise these under
appropriate headings.

Literature does not exist in an aesthetic vacuum, however,
and you should try to find out as much as possible about the
context of its production and reception. It is particularly important to read other works by the same author and writings by
contemporaries. At this early stage, you may want to restrict
your secondary reading to those standard reference works, such
as biographies, which are widely available in public libraries. In

the long run, however, it pays to read as wide a range of critical studies as possible.

Some students, and tutors, worry that such studies may stifle the development of any truly personal response. But this won't happen if you are alert to the danger and read critically. After all, you wouldn't passively accept what a stranger told you in conversation. The fact that a critic's views are in print does not necessarily make them any more authoritative (as a glance at the review pages of the *TLS* and *London Review of Books* will reveal). So question the views you find: 'Does this critic's interpretation agree with mine and where do we part company?' 'Can it be right to try and restrict this text's meanings to those found by its author or first audience?' 'Doesn't this passage treat a theatrical text as though it were a novel?' Often it is views which you reject which prove most valuable since they challenge you to articulate your own position with greater clarity. Be sure to keep careful notes on what the critic wrote, and your *reactions* to what the critic wrote.

Analyse the question

You cannot begin to answer a question until you understand what task it is you have been asked to perform. Re-cast the question in your own words and reconstruct the line of reasoning which lies behind it. Where there is a choice of topics, try to choose the one for which you are best prepared. It would, for example, be unwise to tackle 'How far do you agree that in *Paradise Lost* Milton transformed the epic models he inherited from ancient Greece and Rome?' without a working knowledge of Homer and Virgil (or *Paradise Lost* for that matter!). If you do not already know the works of these authors, the question should spur you on to read more widely — or discourage you from attempting it at all. The scope of an essay, however, is not always so obvious and you must remain alert to the implied demands of each question. How could you possibly 'Consider the view that *Wuthering Heights* transcends the conventions of the Gothic novel' without reference to at least some of those works which, the question suggests, have *not* transcended Gothic conventions?

When you have decided on a topic, analyse the terms of the question itself. Sometimes these self-evidently require careful definition: *tragedy* and *irony*, for example, are notoriously difficult concepts to pin down and you will probably need to consult a good dictionary of literary terms. Don't ignore, however, those seemingly innocuous phrases which often smuggle in significant assumptions. 'Does Macbeth lack the nobility of the true tragic hero?' obviously invites you to discuss nobility and the nature of the tragic hero. But what of 'lack' and 'true' — do they suggest that the play would be improved had Shakespeare depicted Macbeth in a different manner? or that tragedy is superior to other forms of drama? Remember that you are not expected meekly to agree with the assumptions implicit in the question. Some questions are deliberately provocative in order to stimulate an engaged response. Don't be afraid to take up the challenge.

Sketch out your preliminary ideas

'Which comes first, the evidence or the answer?' is one of those chicken and egg questions. How can you form a view without inspecting the evidence? But how can you know which evidence is relevant without some idea of what it is you are looking for? In practice the mind reviews evidence and formulates preliminary theories or hypotheses at one and the same time, although for the sake of clarity we have separated out the processes. Remember that these early ideas are only there to get you started. You *expect* to modify them in the light of the evidence you uncover. Your initial hypothesis may be an instinctive 'gut-reaction'. Or you may find that you prefer to 'sleep on the problem', allowing ideas to gell over a period of time. Don't worry in either case. The mind is quite capable of processing a vast amount of accumulated evidence, the product of previous reading and thought, and reaching sophisticated intuitive judgements. Eventually, however, you are going to have to think carefully through any ideas you arrive at by such intuitive processes. Are they logical? Do they take account of all the relevant factors? Do they fully answer the question set? Are there any obvious reasons to qualify or abandon them?

Assemble your evidence

Now is the time to return to the text and re-read it with the question and your working hypothesis firmly in mind. Many of the notes you have already made are likely to be useful, but assess the precise relevance of this material and make notes on any new evidence you discover. The important thing is to cast your net widely and take into account points which tend to undermine your case as well as those that support it. As always, ensure that your notes are full, accurate, and reflect your own critical judgements.

You may well need to go outside the text if you are to do full justice to the question. If you think that the 'Oedipus complex' may be relevant to an answer on *Hamlet* then read Freud and a balanced selection of those critics who have discussed the appropriateness of applying psychoanalytical theories to the interpretation of literature. Their views can most easily be tracked down by consulting the annotated bibliographies held by most major libraries (and don't be afraid to ask a librarian for help in finding and using these). Remember that you go to works of criticism not only to obtain information but to stimulate you into clarifying your own position. And that since life is short and many critical studies are long, judicious use of a book's index and/or contents list is not to be scorned. You can save yourself a great deal of future labour if you carefully record full bibliographic details at this stage.

Once you have collected the evidence, organise it coherently. Sort the detailed points into related groups and identify the quotations which support these. You must also assess the relative importance of each point, for in an essay of limited length it is essential to establish a firm set of priorities, exploring some ideas in depth while discarding or subordinating others.

Test your ideas

As we stressed earlier, a hypothesis is only a proposal, and one that you fully expect to modify. Review it with the evidence before you. Do you really still believe in it? It would be surprising if you did not want to modify it in some way. If you cannot see any problems, others may. Try discussing your ideas with friends and relatives. Raise them in class discussions. Your tutor is certain to welcome your initiative. The critical process is essentially collaborative and there is absolutely no reason why you should not listen to and benefit from the views of others. Similarly, you should feel free to test your ideas against the theories put forward in academic journals and books. But do not just borrow what you find. Critically analyse the views on offer and, where appropriate, integrate them into your own pattern of thought. You must, of course, give full acknowledgement to the sources of such views.

Do not despair if you find you have to abandon or modify significantly your initial position. The fact that you are prepared to do so is a mark of intellectual integrity. Dogmatism is never an academic virtue and many of the best essays explore the *process* of scholarly enquiry rather than simply record its results.

Plan your argument

Once you have more or less decided on your attitude to the question (for an answer is never really 'finalised') you have to present your case in the most persuasive manner. In order to do this you must avoid meandering from point to point and instead produce an organised argument — a structured flow of ideas and supporting evidence, leading logically to a conclusion which fully answers the question. Never begin to write until you have produced an outline of your argument.

You may find it easiest to begin by sketching out its main stages as a flow chart or some other form of visual presentation. But eventually you should produce a list of paragraph topics. The paragraph is the conventional written demarcation for a unit of thought and you can outline an argument quite simply by briefly summarising the substance of each paragraph and then checking that these points (you may remember your English teacher referring to them as topic sentences) really do follow a coherent order. Later you will be able to elaborate on each topic, illustrating and qualifying it as you go along. But you will find this far easier to do if you possess from the outset a clear map of where you are heading.

All questions require some form of an argument. Even so-called 'descriptive' questions *imply* the need for an argument. An adequate answer to the request to 'Outline the role of Iago in *Othello*' would do far more than simply list his appearances on stage. It would at the very least attempt to provide some *explanation* for his actions — is he, for example, a representative stage 'Machiavel'? an example of pure evil, 'motiveless malignity'? or a realistic study of a tormented personality reacting to identifiable social and psychological pressures?

Your conclusion ought to address the terms of the question. It may seem obvious, but 'how far do you agree', 'evaluate', 'consider', 'discuss', etc, are *not* interchangeable formulas and your conclusion must take account of the precise wording of the question. If asked 'How far do you agree?', the concluding paragraph of your essay really should state whether you are in complete agreement, total disagreement, or, more likely, partial agreement. Each preceding paragraph should have a clear justification for its existence and help to clarify the reasoning which underlies your conclusion. If you find that a paragraph serves no good purpose (perhaps merely summarising the plot), do not hesitate to discard it.

The arrangement of the paragraphs, the overall strategy of the argument, can vary. One possible pattern is dialectical: present the arguments in favour of one point of view (**thesis**); then turn to counter-arguments or to a rival interpretation (**antithesis**); finally evaluate the competing claims and arrive at your own conclusion (**synthesis**). You may, on the other hand, feel so convinced of the merits of one particular case that you wish to devote your entire essay to arguing that viewpoint persuasively (although it is always desirable to indicate, however briefly, that you are aware of alternative, if flawed, positions). As the essays contained in this volume demonstrate, there are many other possible strategies. Try to adopt the one which will most comfortably accommodate the demands of the question and allow you to express your thoughts with the greatest possible clarity.

Be careful, however, not to apply abstract formulas in a mechanical manner. It is true that you should be careful to define your terms. It is *not* true that every essay should begin with 'The dictionary defines x as . . .'. In fact, definitions are often best left until an appropriate moment for their introduction arrives. Similarly every essay should have a beginning, middle and end. But it does not follow that in your opening paragraph you should announce an intention to write an essay, or that in your concluding paragraph you need to signal an imminent desire to put down your pen. The old adages are often useful reminders of what constitutes good practice, but they must be interpreted intelligently.

Write out the essay

Once you have developed a coherent argument you should aim to communicate it in the most effective manner possible. Make certain you clearly identify yourself, and the question you are answering. Ideally, type your answer, or at least ensure your handwriting is legible and that you leave sufficient space for your tutor's comments. Careless presentation merely distracts from the force of your argument. Errors of grammar, syntax and spelling are far more serious. At best they are an irritating blemish, particularly in the work of a student who should be sensitive to the nuances of language. At worst, they seriously confuse the sense of your argument. If you are aware that you have stylistic problems of this kind, ask your tutor for advice at the earliest opportunity. Everyone, however, is liable to commit the occasional howler. The only remedy is to give yourself plenty of time in which to proof-read your manuscript (often reading it aloud is helpful) before submitting it.

Language, however, is not only an instrument of communication; it is also an instrument of thought. If you want to think clearly and precisely you should strive for a clear, precise prose style. Keep your sentences short and direct. Use modern, straightforward English wherever possible. Avoid repetition, clichés and wordiness. Beware of generalisations, simplifications, and overstatements. Orwell analysed the relationship between stylistic vice and muddled thought in his essay 'Politics and the English Language' (1946) — it remains essential reading (and is still readily available in volume 4 of the Penguin *Collected Essays, Journalism and Letters*). Generalisations, for example, are always dangerous. They are rarely true and tend to suppress the individuality of the texts in question. A remark such as 'Keats always employs sensuous language in his poetry' is not only fatuous (what, after all, does it mean? is *every* word he wrote equally 'sensuous'?) but tends to obscure interesting distinctions which could otherwise be made between, say, the descriptions in the 'Ode on a Grecian Urn' and those in 'To Autumn'.

The intelligent use of quotations can help you make your points with greater clarity. Don't sprinkle them throughout your essay without good reason. There is no need, for example, to use them to support uncontentious statements of fact. 'Macbeth murdered Duncan' does not require textual evidence (unless you wish to dispute Thurber's brilliant parody, 'The Macbeth Murder Mystery', which reveals Lady Macbeth's father as the culprit!). Quotations should be included, however, when they are necessary to support your case. The proposition that Macbeth's imaginative powers wither after he has killed his king would certainly require extensive quotation: you would almost certainly want to analyse key passages from both before and after the murder (perhaps his first and last soliloquies?). The key word here is 'analyse'. Quotations cannot make your points on their own. It is up to you to demonstrate their relevance and clearly explain to your readers *why* you want them to focus on the passage you have selected.

Most of the academic conventions which govern the presentation of essays are set out briefly in the style sheet below. The question of gender, however, requires fuller discussion. More than half the population of the world is female. Yet many writers still refer to an undifferentiated *man*kind. Or write of the author and *his* public. We do not think that this convention has much to recommend it. At the very least, it runs the risk of introducing unintended sexist attitudes. And at times leads to such patent absurdities as 'Cleopatra's final speech asserts *man*'s true nobility'. With a little thought, you can normally find ways of expressing yourself which do not suggest that the typical author, critic or reader is male. Often you can simply use plural forms, which is probably a more elegant solution than relying on such awkward formulations as 's/he' or 'he and she'. You should also try to avoid distinguishing between male and female authors on the basis of forenames. Why *Jane* Austen and not *George* Byron? Refer to all authors by their last names unless there is some good reason not to. Where there may otherwise be confusion, say between T S and George Eliot, give the name in full when if first occurs and thereafter use the last name only.

Finally, keep your audience firmly in mind. Tutors and examiners are interested in understanding your conclusions and the processes by which you arrived at them. They are not interested in reading a potted version of a book they already know. **So don't pad out your work with plot summary.**

Hints for examinations

In an examination you should go through exactly the same processes as you would for the preparation of a term essay. The only difference lies in the fact that some of the stages will have had to take place before you enter the examination room. This should not bother you unduly. Examiners are bound to avoid the merely eccentric when they come to formulate papers and if you have read widely and thought deeply about the central issues raised by your set texts you can be confident you will have sufficient material to answer the majority of questions sensibly.

The fact that examinations impose strict time limits makes it *more* rather than less, important that you plan carefully. There really is no point in floundering into an answer without any idea of where you are going, particularly when there will not be time to recover from the initial error.

Before you begin to answer any question at all, study the entire paper with care. Check that you understand the rubric and know how many questions you have to answer and whether any are compulsory. It may be comforting to spot a title you feel confident of answering well, but don't rush to tackle it: read *all* the questions before deciding which *combination* will allow you to display your abilities to the fullest advantage. Once you have made your choice, analyse each question, sketch out your ideas, assemble the evidence, review your initial hypothesis, plan your argument, *before* trying to write out an answer. And make notes at each stage: not only will these help you arrive at a sensible conclusion, but examiners are impressed by evidence of careful thought.

Plan your time as well as your answers. If you have practised writing timed essays as part of your revision, you should not find this too difficult. There can be a temptation to allocate extra time to the questions you know you can answer well; but this is always a short-sighted policy. You will find yourself left to face a question which would in any event have given you difficulty without even the time to give it serious thought. It is, moreover, easier to gain marks at the lower end of the scale than at the upper, and you will never compensate for one poor answer by further polishing two satisfactory answers. Try to leave some time at the end of the examination to re-read your answers and correct any obvious errors. If the worst comes to the worst and you run short of time, don't just keep writing until you are forced to break off in mid-paragraph. It is far better to provide for the examiner a set of notes which indicate the overall direction of your argument.

Good luck — but if you prepare for the examination conscientiously and tackle the paper in a methodical manner, you won't need it!

(annotation) long verse quotation, indented and introduced by a colon. Quotation marks are not needed.

(annotation) book/play title given in italics. In a handwritten or typed manuscript this would appear as underlining: <u>Twelfth Night</u>.

(annotation) Line references are normally given directly after the quotation, in brackets.

(annotation) Short verse quotation incorporated into the text of the essay within quotation marks. Line endings are indicated by a slash (/).

(annotation) Three dots (ellipsis) indicate where words or phrases have been cut from a quotation or when (as here) a quotation begins mid-sentence.

---

animal. Orsino however, tells of his infatuation and the torment he experiences in terms which are unusually savage:

> That instant was I turned into a hart,
> And my desires, like fell and cruel hounds,
> E'er since pursue me.
>
> (I.1.22–24)

Right from the beginning, when Viola says that she'll go and serve Orsino, the language suggests not so much playfulness, as an element of violence against her own sexual identity: 'I'll serve this Duke./ Thou shalt present me as an eunuch to him' (I.2.56–57).

Sexuality, the underlying theme of so much of *Twelfth Night*, is, as these two quotations illustrate, frequently described in menacing, predatory terms. Sexual attraction, as a motivating force in the play, is common to all. Even Sir Toby ends up marrying Maria. But it is also an area in which norms, as in carnival, are again turned upside-down. For desire takes, during the action if not the conclusion, little notice of what sex anyone is. Antonio, the sea-captain, follows his master Sebastian around with passionate devotion: 'I could not stay behind you. My desire,/ More sharp than filèd steel, did spur me forth' (III.3.4–5). Sir Andrew Aguecheek has only to see the unfortunate Viola, in the guise of Cesario, talking to Olivia and he challenges him to a duel. At the centre of the story, although Olivia has sworn, in melodramatic fashion enough, that as a form of mourning her brother, she's going to give up all contact with men:

> . . . like a cloistress she will veilèd walk,
> And water once a day her chamber round
> With eye-offending brine
>
> (I.1.30–32)

irrationally smitten on her first meeting with Cesario— — 'Even so quickly may one catch the plague?' (I.5.284). distribution of emotional energy across the sexes means, of course, that the language of passion becomes detached from the context of who delivers it and to whom. Just as, in the sub-plot, Maria's bawdy jibes match those of Sir Toby Belch and Sir Andrew, so the language of Cesario–Viola's famous wooing speech to Olivia ('Make me a willow cabin at your gate . . .' —

12

We have divided the following information into two sections. Part A describes those rules which it is essential to master no matter what kind of essay you are writing (including examination answers). Part B sets out some of the more detailed conventions which govern the documentation of essays.

PART A: LAYOUT

Titles of texts

Titles of published books, plays (of any length), long poems, pamphlets and periodicals (including newspapers and magazines), works of classical literature, and films should be underlined: e.g. David Copperfield (novel), Twelfth Night (play), Paradise Lost (long poem), Critical Quarterly (periodical), Horace's Ars Poetica (Classical work), Apocalypse Now (film).

Notice how important it is to distinguish between titles and other names. Hamlet is the play; Hamlet the prince. Wuthering Heights is the novel; Wuthering Heights the house. Underlining is the equivalent in handwritten or typed manuscripts of printed italics. So what normally appears in this volume as *Othello* would be written as Othello in your essay.

Titles of articles, essays, short stories, short poems, songs, chapters of books, speeches, and newspaper articles are enclosed in quotation marks; e.g. 'The Flea' (short poem), 'The Prussian Officer' (short story), 'Middleton's Chess Strategies' (article), 'Thatcher Defects!' (newspaper headline).

Exceptions: Underlining titles or placing them within quotation marks does not apply to sacred writings (e.g. Bible, Koran, Old Testament, Gospels) or parts of a book (e.g. Preface, Introduction, Appendix).

It is generally incorrect to place quotation marks around a title of a published book which you have underlined. The exception is 'titles within titles', e.g. 'Vanity Fair': A Critical Study (title of a book about *Vanity Fair*).

Quotations

Short verse quotations of a single line or part of a line should be incorporated within quotation marks as part of the running text of your essay. Quotations of two or three lines of verse are treated in the same way, with line endings indicated by a slash(/). For example:

1 In <u>Julius Caesar,</u> Antony says of Brutus, 'This was the noblest Roman of them all'.

2 The opening of Antony's famous funeral oration, 'Friends, Romans, Countrymen, lend me your ears;/ I come to bury Caesar not to praise him', is a carefully controlled piece of rhetoric.

Longer verse quotations of more than three lines should be indented from the main body of the text and introduced in most cases with a colon. Do not enclose indented quotations within quotation marks. For example:

It is worth pausing to consider the reasons Brutus gives to justify his decision to assassinate Caesar:

> It must be by his death; and for my part,
> I know no personal cause to spurn at him,
> But for the general. He would be crowned.
> How might that change his nature, there's the question.

At first glance his rationale may appear logical . . .

Prose quotations of less than three lines should be incorporated in the text of the essay, within quotation marks. Longer prose quotations should be indented and the quotation marks omitted. For example:

1 Before his downfall, Caesar rules with an iron hand. His political opponents, the Tribunes Marullus and Flavius, are 'put to silence' for the trivial offence of 'pulling scarfs off Caesar's image'.

2 It is interesting to note the rhetorical structure of Brutus's Forum speech:

> Romans, countrymen, and lovers, hear me for my cause, and be silent that you may hear. Believe me for my honour, and have respect to mine honour that you may believe. Censure me in your wisdom, and awake your senses, that you may the better judge.

Tenses: When you are relating the events that occur within a work of fiction or describing the author's technique, it is the convention to use the present tense. Even though Orwell published *Animal Farm* in 1945, the book *describes* the animals' seizure of Manor Farm. Similarly, Macbeth always *murders* Duncan, despite the passage of time.

PART B: DOCUMENTATION

When quoting from verse of more than twenty lines, provide line references: e.g. In 'Upon Appleton House' Marvell's mower moves 'With whistling scythe and elbow strong' (l.393).

Quotations from plays should be identified by act, scene and line references: e.g. Prospero, in Shakespeare's The Tempest, refers to Caliban as 'A devil, a born devil' (IV.1.188). (i.e. Act 4. Scene 1. Line 188).

Quotations from prose works should provide a chapter reference and, where appropriate, a page reference.

Bibliographies should list full details of all sources consulted. The way in which they are presented varies, but one standard format is as follows:

1 Books and articles are listed in alphabetical order by the author's last name. Initials are placed after the surname.
2 If you are referring to a chapter or article within a larger work, you list it by reference to the author of the article or chapter, not the editor (although the editor is also named in the reference).
3 Give (in parentheses) the place and date of publication, e.g. (London, 1962). These details can be found within the book itself. Here are some examples:

> Brockbank, J.P., 'Shakespeare's Histories, English and Roman', in Ricks, C. (ed.) English Drama to 1710 (Sphere History of Literature in the English Language) (London, 1971).
>
> Gurr, A., 'Richard III and the Democratic Process', Essays in Criticism 24 (1974), pp. 39–47.
>
> Spivack, B., Shakespeare and the Allegory of Evil (New York, 1958).

Footnotes: In general, try to avoid using footnotes and build your references into the body of the essay wherever possible. When you do use them give the full bibliographic reference to a work in the first instance and then use a short title: e.g. See K. Smidt, Unconformities in Shakespeare's History Plays (London, 1982), pp. 43–47 becomes Smidt (pp. 43–47) thereafter. Do not use terms such as 'ibid.' or 'op. cit.' unless you are absolutely sure of their meaning.

There is a principle behind all this seeming pedantry. The reader ought to be able to find and check your references and quotations as quickly and easily as possible. Give additional information, such as canto or volume number whenever you think it will assist your reader.

SUGGESTIONS FOR FURTHER READING

Critical Studies

Barber, C L, *Shakespeare's Festive Comedy* (Princeton, NJ, 1959)

Barton, A, '*As You Like It* and *Twelfth Night*: Shakespeare's Sense of an Ending', in Bradbury, M and Palmer, D J (eds), *Shakespearean Comedy* (London, 1972)

Eagleton, T, 'Language and Reality in *Twelfth Night*', in Cox, C B and Palmer, D J (eds), *Shakespeare's Wide and Universal Stage* (Manchester, 1989)

Frye, N, *A Natural Perspective* (New York, 1965)

Greif, K, 'Plays and Playing in *Twelfth Night*', in *Shakespeare Survey* 34 (1981)

Hayles, N, 'Sexual Disguise in *As You Like It* and *Twelfth Night*', in *Shakespeare Survey* 32 (1979)

Kott, J, 'Shakespeare's Bitter Arcadia', in *Shakespeare Our Contemporary* (London, 1965)

Palmer, D J, *Twelfth Night* (Macmillan Casebooks: Basingstoke, 1972)

Potter, L, *Twelfth Night: Text and Performance* (Basingstoke, 1985)

Longman Group UK Limited
*Longman House, Burnt Mill, Harlow, Essex, CM20 2JE, England
and Associated Companies throughout the World.*

First published 1990
ISBN 0 582 06050 8

*Set in 10/12pt Century Schoolbook, Linotron 202
Printed in Great Britain
by Bell and Bain Ltd., Glasgow*

Acknowledgement
The editors would like to thank Zachary Leader for his assistance with
the style sheet.